TEN
RELIGIONS
OF THE EAST

TEN
RELIGIONS
OF THE EAST

Edward Rice

FOUR WINDS PRESS
New York

PHOTO CREDITS

Baha'i National Information Office, p. 141
Consulate General of Japan, New York, pp. 119, 125
New York Public Library Picture Collection, pp. 131, 145
Edward Rice, pp. 7, 19, 43, 63, 73, 74, 140

Illustrations on pp. 25, 39, 79, 88-89, and 93, Courtesy of Edward Rice

Published by Four Winds Press
A division of Scholastic Magazines, Inc., New York, N.Y.
Copyright © 1978 by Edward Rice
All rights reserved
Printed in the United States of America
Library of Congress Catalog Card Number: 78-6186
Book design by Kathleen Westray

2   3   4   5   82   81   80

Library of Congress Cataloging in Publication Data
Rice, Edward.
Ten religions of the East.
Includes index.
Summary: Discusses ten faiths that have originated in the East: Bon, Sikhism, Taoism. [etc.]
1. Religions—Juvenile literature. [1. Religions]
I. Title.
BL92.R5   291   78-6186
ISBN 0-590-07473-3

CONTENTS

INTRODUCTION

This volume is a continuation of my book *The Five Great Religions*, which deals with Hinduism, Buddhism, Judaism, Islam and Christianity. These five number as members the majority of the world's peoples, even in lands where religion may be proscribed, such as the various socialist and communist nations, for religious yearnings have a way of surviving and surfacing despite the most stringent efforts of governments to efface them.

In addition to the five great faiths there are numerous others, some of the utmost importance despite the small number of adherents and practitioners. Some may have only a few million members, others may be so isolated that they are virtually unknown in the West. Still others may be known merely by hearsay and vague references. Yet they have great vitality, and often have had a wide influence upon the world. The faith of the ancient Iranian prophet Zoroaster (sixth century B.C.), for example, not only had a direct influence upon the Jews of the Babylonian exile, and

[1]

through Judaism upon the later doctrines of the Christian churches, but at one point influenced or gave birth to other religions, ways and paths which have since disappeared. Today Zoroastrianism is the faith for barely 140,000 souls, yet at the time Christianity was born, virtually the entire "civilized" world, except for the Jews and a few other small groups outside India and the Far East, was to some extent either Zoroastrian or influenced by the Prophet's doctrines, though perhaps in a perverted form. One might point out a more contemporary example, the Jains of India, a sect of about three million members. Once a powerful faith that influenced the greater Ways of Hinduism and Buddhism and was noted as the preserver of the scriptures, epics and sciences of its larger neighbors, Jainism might have languished in the footnotes of history had it not been for the fact that one of its primary doctrines, that of ahimsa, or nonviolence, was taken up by Mohandas K. Gandhi, a Hindu, as a means of ousting the British from colonial India. By persuading Indians in general, the more aggressive Muslims as well as his own Hindu people, to be nonviolent in the face of well-armed British soldiers, Gandhi put the violence of an occupying power into a perspective that not only shocked the British themselves but provided a profound lesson for the rest of the world. But the lesson of ahimsa (which Gandhi translated as "soul force") did not end there. In the United States the late Dr. Martin Luther King, Jr., took up nonviolence as a tool (one hesitates to call it a "weapon") in the struggle to end racial discrimination and to help bring American blacks to full civil freedom. Nonviolence—ahimsa—is now a part of political life, practiced from time to time, and certainly to be considered as one of the alternatives to physical force in opposing a more powerful enemy.

This book concentrates on faiths that have originated in the East, though some of them, like Theosophy and the Baha'i Faith, are now practiced primarily by Westerners. But these too, have

Oriental roots—Hindu and Buddhist in the case of Theosophy,
Islamic in the case of Baha'i. I treat also an ancient, obscure
Tibetan religion known as Bon, which leads a shadowy life under
the more powerful form of Buddhism the Tibetans practice, and a
fairly recent faith, Sikhism, which developed as a need to follow a
more peaceful way—one of Devotion—between warring Muslims
and Hindus in western India. Among the very ancient paths are
Taoism and Confucianism—both Chinese—two old ways, con-
tradictory and even hostile to each other, which form a kind of
synthesis of the Chinese character and soul. These two faiths
were heavily influenced by Buddhism and by many underlying
layers of animistic, shamanistic folk beliefs and superstitions.
Shinto is a gentle nature faith of the ancient Japanese which has
so influenced our thinking about Japan today. Much of what the
West admires in Japan—the calm appreciation of nature, of a few
rocks, a small pond, a leaf on a path, a fringe of trees against a
winter snow, the ability to make the most of a few natural
objects—is the result of the Japanese people's age-old veneration
for the spirits that inhabit the countryside, the skies, the elements and the home and garden. And then there is the curious
sect known as Cao Dai in Southeast Asia, which was begun by
two rather shady characters and changed into a world-vision of
some insight. The development of Cao Dai was frustrated by the
Vietnam war and subsequent events, but its founders had a vision
in which they combined with notable success the world's great
faiths into one new syncretist movement.

It may be necessary to point out that the adherents of all the
faiths I write about are all too human: that the average Jain, Sikh,
Shintoist, Confucian, etc., is no more saintly in his or her daily
life than the average churchgoer in our own community. There
are saints and sinners everywhere. The Jain who violates his
community's proscriptions against certain practices, who, for
example, becomes violent, is just as human (and sinful) as the

[3]

Christian or Jew who does not follow the Ten Commandments. In all too many cases, rituals, ceremonies and customs (such as those involving birth, initiatory rites into the religious community, marriage and death), rules and regulations about food and clothing—the superficials—are what people may follow scrupulously, while conveniently ignoring the more important teachings about honesty, morality, probity, prayer, self-analysis and meditation—the true religious life. Yet the writer tries to show what the ideal is, what one must strive for, not what one can fall to. Otherwise the description of any community would be one long litany of faults and complaints. In the end, we can hope that mankind exhausts the karmic cycle of birth and rebirth—however the individual chooses to define his or her self in the playing out of the universe—and emerges a saint, an enlightened, liberated soul.

1

THE JAINS

Myth and legend abound in virtually every religion. The Jains, that strange and enigmatic sect of India, have some fascinating myths, in which some hard kernels of truth may be discovered. The Jains, who number not quite three million members out of India's six hundred million people, still represent one of the most celebrated and most influential of the faiths of the subcontinent, though many of their practices, beliefs and customs are erroneously ascribed to the Hindus—among them the monks' habit of wearing cloth masks to avoid inhaling insects, or of going about stark naked as a means of expressing their liberation from all worldly things. Many of the unclothed holy men one sees or hears of in India are not Hindus but are members of a branch of the Jains, the Digambaras, or Sky Clad.

Jainism is possibly the only faith in the world to take seriously the injunction not to kill. Though virtually every religion has such a prohibition, an amazing number of loopholes are always found to negate the commandment. Even Hinduism, so strict in many ways, allows people of certain castes to serve as warriors, or to kill animals or eat flesh meats. Few Hindus are as scrupulous as the Jains in not injuring harmless insects. Though the majority of Buddhists are strict about not killing animals, as well as people, others either ignore the prohibition (as do the Tibetans and the tantrics) or merely observe it when practical, the Japanese being a noted example.

Of the great myths, we may start with that of the legendary founder, the first Jain, Rsabha, otherwise the Bull, who represents morality. Rsabha is the righteous king, and an incarnation of the great Hindu preserver, the Lord Vishnu; though he is the original Jain, he is also a minor Hindu deity. He was one of the sons of the god Nabhi (whose name means navel); his mother was Meru, the Axial Mountain, on which the Indian subcontinent and thus the world is centered. Jain and Hindu traditions do not quite match. The Hindus, in their oldest texts, some previous to the seventh and eighth centuries B.C., say that Rsabha, after teaching his sons the path of wisdom, abandoned his kingdom to show that the Way must be put into practice and retired to a mountain cave to engage in austerities so fearsome that he became but an "agglomeration of skin and fibers." But the Jains state that Rsabha and the other early Jain saints and leaders preceded the gods of Hinduism; Jainism is therefore the oldest faith in the land.

The early Jain leaders are known as tirthankaras, or "ford crossers"—that is, they have crossed the stream of existence into the land of liberation and have become kevalins, or "completed souls." Thus they are freed from the endless rounds of birth and rebirth that bind mankind. The first twenty-two tirthankaras (there are twenty-four in all) are said to be big and long-lived. Rsabha, the first, was born in the legendary aeons when the golden age of the cosmos was running down and the world was entering the present period of wars, social unrest, disease,

In Gwalior state, once a Jain center, rows of huge statues of the tirthankaras have been carved in a roadside cliff. Most of the statues, which
show the Jain saints "Sky Clad," have been damaged by Muslim invaders
in past centuries.

famine, natural disasters and the other problems that plague an unhappy and distraught mankind. He was believed to have lived 8,400,000 years (the number 84, in whatever combination, is mystical) and was five hundred poles in height (we cannot be sure of the length of a pole in ancient times).

Uncounted millennia later, as the tirthankaras declined in span of life and height, the twenty-third tirthankara, Parsva, was born. He lived a mere one hundred years; he was also of ordinary human size. He was most likely a historical figure, for some acceptable facts are known about him. Jain sources state that he was born in 817 B.C. in the sacred city of Benares, on the Ganges River in eastern India. He was of the kshatriya, or warrior caste. As a child he was known to be remarkably intelligent, kind and courageous, and a number of stories tell of these qualities. He gained a reputation as a fearless warrior, but at thirty he renounced the worldly life to become an ascetic. During eighty-four concentrated days (note the mystical number) during which he fasted, prayed and practiced austerities, he gained enlightenment, becoming, like the other tirthankaras, a kevalin, a "Completed Soul." Disciples, both men and women, flocked to Parsva, who organized them into a number of communities. He preached for seventy years, and at the end of this time, having broken through the karmic chains that bind all men, he retired to a mountain in Bengal, in eastern India, to shed his body so that his soul, now liberated from all earthly bonds, could escape the world.

Parsva had enjoined his followers to honor four binding vows: 1) not to take any form of life, 2) not to lie, 3) not to steal, 4) not to own property. The last by implication included vows of chastity and celibacy, two rules not normally binding upon people in ancient India, where the family was the center of life. After Parsva's death his teachings were carried on by his followers in eastern India, where they were to be taken up by the family of a man called Vardhamana, the twenty-fourth and last tirthankara.

Vardhamana is credited with being the founder of the Jains, though obviously the sect had been in existence before him, though to what extent no one can be sure. He was born in the area now called Bihar, in eastern India. He was a contemporary of the better-known Gautama Buddha, who was also a native of the same region. Like Buddha, Vardhamana was a member of the warrior caste, a kshatriya, and a prince who left the royal palace for the life of the mendicant saint. As in the case of many ancient figures, though historical, the dates of birth and death are open to dispute. Some sources state that Vardhamana lived from 599 to 527 B.C., and other authorities set the dates at 530 to 468 B.C., while the Jains themselves prefer 610 to 538 B.C. Yet they celebrated the 2,500th anniversary of Vardhamana's "nirvana" (that is, attainment of freedom from earthly bonds) in the year beginning November 13, 1974, which would mean he died in 526 B.C.

Like Parsva, Vardhamana was intelligent, courageous and kind. His parents gave him the best education a young prince could have. Eventually he was married to the daughter of a neighboring prince. Her name was Yasoda (or Jasoda), and they had a daughter, Priyadarsana. This is the tradition of the less strict of the Jain movements, the Svetambaras. Their rivals, the more rigorous Digambaras, state unequivocally that Vardhamana was celibate. Whatever the situation, there came a point when, not finding the peace of mind he desired in the court, the prince decided to abandon the life of the palace to become a wandering monk. When he was about twenty-eight, his parents died. As members of the community founded by Parsva, they had followed one of his teachings to the letter, which stated that when a person reached a certain high level of spiritual accomplishment, it was a logical step to end his or her own life. This was often done by starvation. Consequently, the king and queen, by this means, moved on to the blessedness of the eternal.

Vardhamana's next step tells us something of the formality and rigidity of Indian life. Though he wanted to follow an ascetic way, he had to ask permission from his elder brother, and had to wait two years before the brother agreed. Vardhamana was now thirty.

For the formal ceremony of divestiture of his royal role, Vardhamana went to a park outside the city of Vaisali, where a group of monks supported by his clan (such is the supposition) had their center. Here, under a huge asoka tree, whose leaves never know either grief or pain, Vardhamana fasted for two and a half days, watched by a huge crowd of several thousand people, including monks and householders (as lay people are often called in India). Then he took the vow that would lead to the life of the monk. "The young aspirant cut off with his own hands his beautiful locks of hair and then laid aside his rich robes and the insignia of the warrior caste. The tears of his beautiful wife and affectionate daughter could not bind him," wrote one of his biographers. From that time on "he had to observe the virtues of non-injury, truth and continence. He was to tread the path of liberation from sorrows and happiness and remain equally indifferent to life and death. He now led the life of a wandering monk." He gave away his last bit of clothing to "roam about in the majesty of Nature."

In such a state, Vardhamana, whom we will now call by his better-known name, Mahavir, or the Great Man (the name commonly used by the Jains), spent twelve years wandering from place to place, in heat, cold and rain. He never slept more than three hours each night. He fasted, to the point of emaciation. He practiced other austerities, renunciation and self-control, taught the doctrine of nonviolence, or ahimsa, to those who would listen, and engaged in much meditation and self-analysis.

Though he seemed to have met and preached to many people, he did not at first make many converts. One of them, according to the Jains, was a man called Makkali Gosala, who considered himself a tirthankara. Gosala was the founder of the Ajivika sect, which soon became one of the most important rivals to both the

[10]

Jains and the Buddhists; though it is little known now, it survived until about A.D. 1400. Gosala believed that Fate rules all. Unlike Mahavir, who believed implicitly that man's own good deeds affect his birth and rebirth in future lives, Gosala said that no matter what one did or didn't do, it had no effect on future births. "All beings," he said, "are without power, strength or virtue, but are developed by destiny, chance and nature." Virtuous conduct, vows to the gods, penances and chastity cannot change a person's destiny. "Just as a ball of thread will, when thrown, unwind to its full length, so fool and wise alike will take their course, and make an end of sorrow."

Gosala's teacher had been even more pessimistic. He was Ajita, otherwise called the Man with the Hair Blanket by some and the Man with the Blanket and a Mule by others. Ajita believed that good or bad deeds, evil, charity, compassion were all irrelevant in the end. The body dissolved into the primary elements at death, no matter what had been done.

Mahavir, after six years of philosophical dispute, in which he could not convince his companion and opponent that salvation came through one's own efforts, broke with him. Alone again, he endured a number of incidents. He was tortured by forest hunters, but would not cry out in pain, for he had taken a vow of silence. Near a town he was arrested for being a thief and beaten, then ordered to be hanged. Seven times the noose was placed around his neck; seven times it slipped as he was hoisted up. The officials finally released him on the obvious deduction that Mahavir was a great soul. Other incidents occurred, which need not be detailed. At the end of twelve years, having undergone the fasts, austerities and prayers which seem to be prescribed for such holy men, Mahavir came to a small village with the name of Jambia. Here he sat under a sal tree to meditate. It was at this point that he reached his final state, that of ultimate knowledge. After two days he became a kevalin, a "completed soul," and a Jina, a "conqueror." He had realized ultimate knowledge, had realized everything—the mystery of God, human beings, animals and their thought currents; he had solved the secrets of creation and of the cosmos. He had become a tirthankara, a truth seeker and a pathfinder.

Now he was truly able to appear before the public and to be heard. He preached the realization of the eternal as the privilege of all mankind, not of only a few, as the Hindu priests taught. This was a radical break, for, like the Lord Buddha, who was to come soon afterward, he taught that salvation was possible not only for the select but also for the masses. Rank, privilege, caste, wealth, gifts to the priests, sacrifices—all meant nothing, for the individual could, by following the Way proclaimed by Mahavir, attain his own salvation. By leading the proper life on earth, all the sins of one's past lives can be overcome, destroyed. Repentance of sins, austerities, self-discipline and the control of the senses lead one to be free in both mind and body. It was a liberal and universal doctrine, and everyone had the right to practice it.

Mahavir's first converts were probably the monks and householders of the communities that owed their origin to Parsva's teachings. He also made numerous converts among the rich and the royalty, but failed to reach large numbers of the ordinary people, as Buddha would and as his teachings implied. The problem was that much was demanded of the individual, for he must become a Jina, a conqueror, also, and make rather extraordinary demands upon the self. In fact, this theme of Jina, the (self) conqueror, came to be the name of the movement, for that is what "Jain" implies, the person who has conquered.

The central fact in Mahavir's teaching was that the substance known as karma must, in effect, be burned away by prayer, austerities and self-discipline. Karma was and is a common concept in Hinduism, Buddhism and some other Eastern ways, but among the Jains it took a special form. While others saw karma as meaning something like the fruit of past actions, which would produce good or evil results depending on how one behaved, the Jains saw karma as something literal, tangible. It was a substance adhering to the soul, and until it was scrubbed away or burned out, the soul would be hampered by it. The liberated person was one who had not only overcome karma but had, in a literal sense, destroyed it. There could be no such thing as "good" karma. Ideally, there must be no karma at all. And then one was freed of the prison of birth and rebirth.

To help his followers attain liberation, Mahavir gave a more positive form to Parsva's four vows, and added a fifth. These vows, or vratas, are as follows:

Ahimsa: not to destroy life through carelessness; to be non-violent.

Satya: to speak only what is true, pleasant and good.

Asteya: to take nothing which is not freely given.

Brahmacarya: to practice celibacy.

Aparigraha: to own no worldly possessions.

The five vratas are clearly more easily followed by the monk than by the householder, but the laity usually do what they can to observe them. Of the five, the most important is that of ahimsa, an ancient doctrine which probably originated centuries before Parsva and Mahavir adopted it, and which has had a profound effect upon all of India. Jain monks will not eat after dark for fear an insect might fall into their food and be killed. Water is strained several times to guard the tiny insects that might be present. Face masks keep other insects from being inhaled. Foods which may be considered "alive"—potatoes, for example—cannot be taken; in fact, all foods must be examined so that the eater can be sure they are free from animal life. A Jain cannot be a farmer, again for fear of killing creatures in the soil; the result is that most Jains enter business or a profession. A Jain's entire life is circumspect and regulated. Violent motions are forbidden: a quick movement of the arms, legs or body might injure souls in the air; running or stamping one's feet can kill small insects or harm souls in the earth or in stones. A scrupulous Jain will carry a brush with which to clear his path. But this concentration on nonviolence is not to protect others—that is the Buddhist view, and one also developed by Mahatma Gandhi—but to save the individual Jain from karmic debts which would harm him and would have to be burned away.

Though he lacked followers in quantity, those Mahavir attracted were dedicated and sincere. The traditional number of followers is fourteen thousand, though some scholars believe he had as few as nine thousand, and some sources even mention a mere forty-six hundred. He organized them into four groups—monks, nuns, laymen and laywomen. These groups, called tirthas, were divided into nine schools, each under the direction of one of Mahavir's chief disciples. Mahavir taught for thirty years, and then, at the age of seventy-two, he retired to the village of Pavam in Bihar, where, according to tradition, he starved himself to death, as his parents had done, because he had crossed the stream of transmigration, and to live further would have been pointless.

Mahavir was the last of the tirthankaras. After his death the movement was directed by a series of leaders called ganadharas, or "supporters of the community." For a long time, Mahavir's doctrines gained only a small number of disciples; the more egalitarian and less demanding teaching of the Middle Way, the way of the Lord Buddha, was far more popular. The Jains did not achieve any widespread recognition until the end of the fourth century B.C., when the Maurya emperor, Chandragupta, the founder of the greatest line of Indian rulers in the subcontinent's history, became a patron of the movement and died as one of its monks.

[14]

During this period the eleventh ganadhara, a monk named Bradrabahu, led a group of Jains, including the former emperor, to the Deccan mountains of southwest India. The accounts differ as to exactly what initiated the migration. The popular version is that Bradrabahu had a vision of a coming famine, and thought that refuge in a more fertile area was the sensible course until conditions became better. Another version is that Bihar had already experienced thirty years of drought and famine, and that people were starving and had to move. However, not all the Jains migrated. An important leader called Athulabhadra and a number of other monks and householders refused to follow Bradrabahu. Eventually, after conditions in Bihar became normal again, the exiles returned home, to find that the group which had remained behind had seriously corrupted Jain doctrines, making unwarranted changes in practices as well, and worse, had taken to wearing white robes. Horrified by the state of affairs, Bradrabahu went into a self-imposed exile in the Himalayas, the popular retreat of Indian holy men of whatever belief. Here he passed the rest of his life in a cave, fasting and doing penance. He died in Nepal.

The Jains were now in serious trouble. First of all, the community was split into two groups, hostile to each other, and quarreling over both essentials and trivia. The exiles, who claimed to have maintained traditions, called themselves the Digambaras, the "sky clad," for they wore no clothing and were as naked as the twenty-four tirthankaras had been. The others were known as Svetambaras, or "white-clothed." But the major problem was that the only person who knew the Jain scriptures in their entirety—for this was still an age of oral rather than written tradition—was Bradrabahu, meditating in his Himalayan cave. The Svetambaras called a council of the Jains at the royal city of Pataliputra early in the third century B.C.—so far as the date can be determined. Here the white-clothed monks established a canon of the Jain scriptures out of what each man could remember. The reconstruction resulted in two collections of authoritative works—fourteen Purvas, subsequently lost, and eleven Angas, or Limbs. Though the Angas represent doctrines held by the "sky clad," this group rejected the authority of the scriptures assembled by their rivals. Other issues continued to divide one group from the other. The Digambaras refused to accept women as nuns, saying that only men could attain liberation, and that, to be free, a woman had to be reborn a man at a future life. They held that Mahavira never married. Images of the tirthankaras—images were a late development—had to be represented nude and with downcast eyes. A Jain saint, having attained the highest state of all (as kevalin), need not eat to sustain life.

A formal break came about A.D. 80, and since then the two groups have remained more or less apart from each other, though their doctrines, with a few exceptions, are virtually identical. But the Digambaras insist that all Jain scriptures had been lost by the second century A.D., while the Svetambaras claim that a second council, this in A.D. 475, finally fixed the definite form of the eleven Angas, along with some lesser works. Since that time the Svetambaras, who are the larger group, have been strongest in Gujarat and Rajasthan, in northwest India, while the Digambaras, now declining, are concentrated in the Deccan, a long mountainous plateau along the southwest coast, and in the old princely state of Mysore. There have been minor schisms throughout the years, the biggest being that of a group called the Lonka, or the Sthankavasi, sect, which protested the veneration paid to images by the Jains of Gujarat. They broke away about A.D. 1450 and re-formed themselves some two hundred years later.

But the internal problems of the Jains did not harm their popularity after the days of the great migration. For a long time Jainism, claiming the allegiance of many of the rajas, was one of the most powerful religious forces in India. Jain thinkers, philosophers, scientists, artists, writers and poets were among the leading lights in the land, and Jain scholars not only preserved their own group's writings but rescued, edited and published many works by other Indians—Hindus and Buddhists—which otherwise would have been lost in the turmoil of the ages.

Unfortunately, Jain scriptures, literature and poetry are barely known outside the community, and are rarely translated. One of the few Jain works to receive any recognition is that unusual didactic south Indian work, *The Ankle Bracelet,* by Prince Ilango Adigal. It is one of the products of a school of writing known as Sangam, which goes back to about 1550 B.C. and ends in the third century A.D. Actually we are concerned with the third Sangam, for the first two, like the tirthankaras, go back to primordial times when the gods were just emerging from the heavenly chaos. The works of the third Sangam refer to an ancient time when a great city existed in a place which sounds like the Indus valley; the city was flooded by the river's waters and had to be abandoned. The works of the Sangam incorporate much primitive material—stories, songs, learning and legend—and synthesize them into various long poems which serve not only to entertain but to teach.

What is interesting is that certain aspects of Jainism—the shape of the statues of the tirthankaras, for example—have been traced by scholars back to the Indus cities, which existed about 2750 to 1700 B.C. Hence the major doctrines of the Jains, codified by Mahavir upon basic tenets enunciated by Parsva, may indeed have had truly ancient origins, perhaps not as primordial as the Jains believe, but early enough to make them the original religion of India—and not Hinduism, as the Hindus, and the world, believe. But it is a moot point whether Hinduism is derived from Jainism or Jainism from Hinduism. What is of great interest is the way in which the Jains see the world, not only

[17]

mankind but every living thing, and beyond that, every inanimate object, for even the grossest stone, the tiniest speck of earth, has its soul.

THE TEACHING OF THE JAINS

There is a certain air of pessimism in the doctrines of this people who seek to be Jinas, or conquerors of the self. "All creation groans together in torment," says one ancient Jain text, for everything—a stone on the road, the water in the river, the dust in the wind, the wind itself—is alive. Everything, no matter how inanimate it might seem to others, contains a soul. And that soul must be respected. All souls are really alike. Consciousness is the essence of the soul, and every soul, from the lowest to the highest, possesses it. Though the souls in the lowest forms of matter seem to be lifeless and inert, unconscious, they only appear so, and will someday pass on to another body, one that is perhaps higher.

The soul itself is formless, but it takes the shape of the body which it inhabits and illuminates. The soul of a flea is as big as the flea itself, and the soul of an elephant is as large as the elephant. Eventually, after a multitude of births and rebirths, the soul will free itself of its karmic bounds and, in a place called akasa, become pure consciousness.

The struggle of the soul to liberate itself is a central concern of Jain doctrine. The sect's philosophical system is highly complex, running from what outsiders would term the most primitive animism, for it sees life in the simplest forms of matter, to the loftiest theology and philosophy, on a level with the highest of all the other religions. The basic teachings are easily understood and practiced by the average householder—who is likely to be better educated and enjoy a higher standard of living than his Hindu neighbor. The more complex teachings, like those of all major religions, are the province of the monks and other ascetics and the philosophers and learned men.

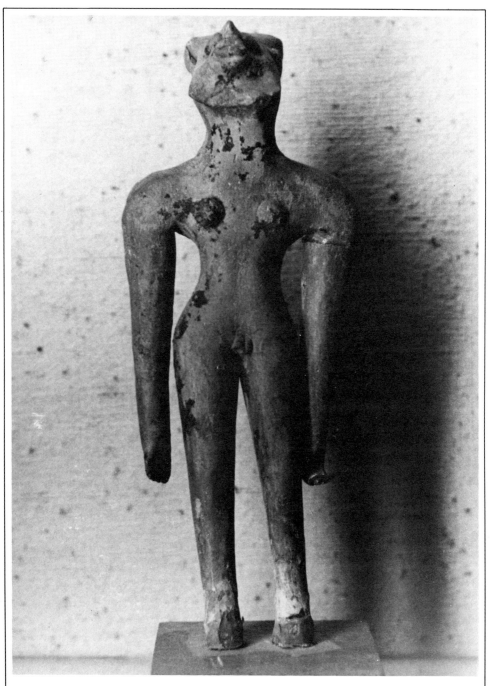

A hermaphroditic figure from the Indus Valley dating back some four thousand years is almost identical in form to Jain statues of later years. Such similarities have led scholars to conclude that Jainism originated in the long-lost cities of Harappa and Mohenjo-Daro, the twin Indus capitals.

Every Jain knows that the universe throbs with life. The most inanimate object—stone, dust or clod of earth—contains a soul so tightly enchained by matter that it cannot escape the foot that kicks it or even cry out in pain. Animals, fish, birds, trees, insects of all types, the iron on the blacksmith's anvil, the fire that melts it—all creation writhes in agony. "An infinite number of times have I been struck and beaten, split and filed," says a Jain verse. "In every kind of existence I have suffered pains which have scarcely known reprieve." Another says, "Many times I have been drawn and quartered, torn apart and skinned . . . killed and scraped, split and gutted . . . stripped of my bark, cut up and sawn into planks."

Therefore the Jain stresses nonviolence, or ahimsa, nonkilling, in the ceaseless effort to keep from destroying even the most rudimentary stages of life, for all lives are but steps in a series of transmigrations of the soul, which is carried by its karma, its accumulation of debts in past lives. Each soul must be reborn one million times. Of these only eight are in human form, though one does not know if this is a blessing or a curse. Even gods, who undergo four hundred thousand rebirths, must pass a life as a man (and not a woman). Consequently life each day is a constant struggle to avoid destruction of souls in whatever form.

The Jains divide life, or matter, into five classes according to the number of senses.

The highest group, with five senses (touch, taste, smell, sight and intelligence), includes gods, men, and the higher animals. Among the latter are monkeys, cattle, horses, parrots, pigeons and snakes—all creatures which play a lively role in Indian folk stories and epics—and the beings in hell.

The second class lacks intelligence but possesses the other four senses. In this group are most large insects, such as flies, wasps and butterflies. The third class, with touch, taste and smell, includes smaller insects—the ants, fleas, bugs and moths, the last being thought to be sightless because of their peculiar habit of flying into flames.

The fourth class, possessing only taste and touch, includes worms, leeches, shellfish and various animalcula. The one-sensed group, with touch alone, is further divided into five groups: vegetation, earth bodies (the earth itself, stones, clay, minerals and jewels—in short, whatever may be found within the earth), water bodies (in whatever form water may come—from oceans and rivers to the rain), fire bodies (which would include lightning as well as various types of flames), and lastly, wind bodies (gases as well as the winds themselves).

Thus the entire cosmos is alive. Whatever is, *is*, possessed of a soul or, rather, inhabited by a soul, groaning, crying, shrieking for release. And even among the lower classes of life there are endless souls: a great tree may possess a single soul but a turnip many. Since a Jain does all within his power not to harm a soul in any form, he must not destroy the things that possess souls. One cannot eat certain types of food, for example, for they have souls, nor light a fire, for that would kill souls in the lighting and burning, nor extinguish a fire, for that would kill the fire's soul. The fire-being may be reborn as a human being in a human body. The man who puts out a fire "kills the fire," says a Jain text. "Thus a wise man who understands the Law should never light a fire." In another passage the same text states, "All things in the universe suffer," so, it counsels, "Live in striving and self-control . . . subduing anger and fear."

Self-control is one of the most prized qualities a Jain may develop. It is necessary not only to avoid taking life but to achieve one's own salvation. One must practice nonviolence, but one must also practice nonattachment. "Enlightened self-interest" is the Jain guide. That is, being free from emotion (either positive or negative) and from dependence on others, being neither pleased nor annoyed with life, having no desires or possessions,

[21]

spurning pleasures. The detached man is the ideal; the passionless man is on the road to salvation. Possessions, treasures, clothing, houses, land, herds of cattle, whatever men work and fight for, crave and dream about are fetters, for in the end a man's "heirs divide it, or workless men steal it, or kings loot it, or it is spoiled or vanishes, or is burned up with his house." Also, to be saved, one must eschew the ties of love, of family and friends, to concentrate on one's own salvation in the upward struggle to rid oneself of karmic particles.

Karma and the karmic particles are the great menace to the Jain. The universe—to reduce a complex metaphysical system to a few basic tenets—is composed of one living, or jiva, substance, and five nonliving, or ajiva, substances. The admixture of jiva and ajiva constitutes the world as it is known to the five senses. Jiva and the ajiva are held together by a kind of elastic, metaphysical glue, which is karma. This is not the abstract karma of the Hindus and the Buddhists, which may be defined briefly as the effect of any action upon the individual, in either a past, present or future life, but an actual substance adhering to the soul. The Jain karma is a subtle though literal substance, which pours into or infiltrates the soul when worldly actions, in a manner of speaking, make a hole in it. This karma creates an actual bondage, the karmic molecules coagulating to form their own kind of body. Now the soul is weighed down by its karma, and unless the individual is careful, the karmic accumulation will grow. The body will eventually die, but the karmic mass will linger on until final liberation.

The means of ridding oneself of this karmic mass is by burning it out, in a sense. Self-restraint and self-discipline are the early steps to take in order to stop the karmic inflow. By self-mortification, austerities, prayer and practices which not everyone is willing to undertake, karma is consumed. Karma is "burned up" in the glow of fasting and penances. Fasting—to death in some cases—is a common austerity. Among the basic practices are rigid control of the senses, speech and mind; confession of faults (practiced by the laity as well as by the monks); reverence to superiors; and good deeds. Serving people but free of the demands of good and evil, the enlightened individual will live in the world. Eventually the soul will transcend the world to attain the perfected state of infinite knowledge and peace. Completely purged of the fetters that karma had imposed, "the soul," says a Jain scripture, "takes the form of a straight line, goes in a single moment without touching anything and taking no space goes upwards [to the place called akasa] and there develops into its natural form, obtains perfection, enlightenment, deliverance and final beatitude and puts an end to all misery."

JAIN METAPHYSICS

So far I have been talking about the general principles of Jain belief, such as any Jain might explain to an outsider. But these principles are supported by a metaphysical system as elaborate as any ever structured by thinking man. Though much of it may seem gloomy and overwhelming—the struggle with karma, for example, which is so intense as to defeat the faint-hearted—there are many positive points of view. The five vows, though stated in negative terms, are actually quite positive. Then, the Jain bases his public conduct on four forms which help promote the commonweal. They are: to perform a kind act without expectation of a reward; to rejoice at the well-being of others; to sympathize with distressed people and to relieve their sufferings; and to pity criminals—an action which few except Jains rarely consider.

The Jains have a passion for categorizing things. Not only are there five vows and four forms, but they see the world divided into three categories—lower, middle and higher. The world is created out of six substances. The universe is divided into two main divisions (sentient beings and nonsentient beings), which interact and cause diversities in the cosmos, which cause evolution. There is an infinite number of living beings occupying the entire space of the universe; these are divided into the free souls (who have thrown off all bondage and are pure, translucent and perfected) and the bound souls, which are seen in two categories, mobile and immobile. All of these are further subdivided.

Then there are the five Gateways of Knowledge, and true philosophy consists of nine principles. The first of them, the soul (I won't detail the others, but they involve numerous categories), is further divided into types, the highest of which possesses ten powers and the lowest four, all of which are subdivided. The soul also possesses perception and intelligence, also subcategorized. The matters that impede the soul's upward progress are also known in many forms. The non-soul is divided into those with form and those without. And so on. Sin is one of the most complex of all Jain subjects. It is the result of moral weakness, and man has a free will not to commit it, or to commit it and suffer. But there are eighteen forms of acts which cause sin, the most heinous of which, as one can expect, is the taking of life of any creature, "living" or "nonliving." Karma, that central concern of the Jain, gets its share of classification, there being nine different types. Karma is removed by ten duties, by the observing of five rules of conduct and by keeping the twelve Great Reflections in mind. Only by following the Three Jewels (Right Faith, Right Knowledge, Right Conduct) can one keep to the path of liberation. On this path one ascends the ladder of fourteen steps, each representing a particular stage of spiritual development. But first one must renounce the five faults.

One could enumerate such lists forever, but they are merely the chapter headings for the metaphysical structure that the Jains have evolved over the centuries. Each category is divided and subdivided, analyzed and studied, taught and followed, so that the man who accomplishes all is truly a perfected soul.

Such is this perfection that the Jains do not believe in a Supreme Power, a One God, such as Jews and Christians do. Since everything possesses the germ of the sacred, there is no creating

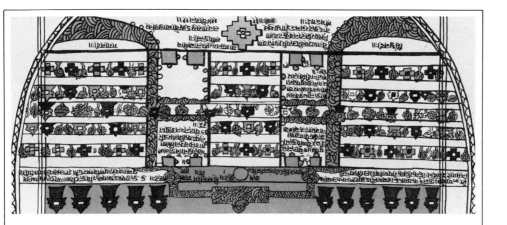

A detail from a late medieval Jain drawing of the universe, showing two of the seven waterways that lead into the oceans. The Jains, like other Indians, viewed the universe as contained within a Cosmic Egg, and crystallized around the mystical Mount Meru, symbol of the ethereal center shared by both the cosmos and the individual.

deity. However, the perfected soul, or the liberated soul, is fit to be worshiped as God. And every soul, no matter how low on the scale of life it might be, is equal to a deity. A contemporary Jain writer (by name, J. Jaini) writes:

> God is only the highest, the noblest and the fullest manifestation of all the powers which lie latent in the soul of man.

> A personal God has no place in Jainism: He is not needed (adds the guru). Jainism has a very definite and uncompromising attitude towards the conception of God. It is accused of being atheistic. This is not so, because Jainism believes in Godhead and in innumerable gods, but certainly Jainism is atheistic in not believing its gods to have created the Universe. Believers in the creation theory make God a man, bringing him down to the level of need and imperfection: whereas Jainism raises a man to Godhead and inspires him to reach as near Godhead as possible by steady faith, right perception, perfect knowledge, and above all, a spotless life.

Because there is no creating power, the world has always existed. Unlike the Hindus and Buddhists, who see a rhythmical cycle of the creation and dissolution of the universe, the Jains believe that it is unchanging and has been unchanged from eternity. Only life on earth is subject to fluctuations. The present period in world life began an infinitely long time ago under ideal conditions, but since the day of Mahavir's Perfection, it has declined. We now live in a second and inferior phase, with conditions worsening each day. This decline will continue over an immense period, until a bottom of the cycle has been reached, after which life on earth will become increasingly better.

WORSHIP

In actual practice the Jains have many rites of their own, among them those that worship the various tirthankaras with hymns and the giving of fruit, flowers and incense, but they may often follow Hindu rites and ceremonies, and some Jains may attend Hindu temples. Though the early Jains rejected the authority of the Hindu Brahmin priests, Jains today often turn to Brahmins for the observance of various rites. They observe virtually the same regulations concerning ritual purity and defilement as the Hindus, perform the same ablutions and recite the same mantras. The ceremonies of marriage, death and so on are similar, if not identical, depending on the type of Jain community. But unlike the Hindus, orthodox Jains take no food between sunset and sunrise for fear of ingesting insects, have no anniversaries to honor the dead, and follow a much more restricted diet than their neighbors. Because they abstain from eating many vegetables and fruits and all forms of meat and other animal food, their diet is severely limited. Vegetables which grow in a bulbous shape — such as onions, eggplant and mushrooms — are forbidden, as are stalks or roots with such a shape. The standard diet is based on rice (a grain which must "die" to be useful as food), milk and milk products and various types of peas or beans.

Festivals in honor of the twenty-four tirthankaras seem to fill the year, and devout Jains will make the pilgrimage to their shrines in Gujarat and elsewhere in western India. The main Jain festival is that of Pujjasana (which means, roughly, "sitting in worship") week, which ends the Jain calendar. During this period, lay people may take the opportunity to live as professed monks. They also gather around the home or the cell of a monk during Pujjasana; they often make a confession of sins to the monk, and beg forgiveness of relatives and friends.

Some old Jain texts have predicted that Jainism will eventually fail in its own land, which may explain the small number of members after so many millennia. Jainism in India has lost its early spirit, and much of what passes for the Jain way today is merely ceremony and custom. Ancient Jain astrological charts have predicted that the initial faith, now so weak, will again be revived, not in India but in the West, where the true doctrines will be properly understood and practiced. The Western center described by the charts is curiously like the United States at the end of the twentieth century.

Jain monks, breaking with their own communities, which do not permit overseas travel because of the bad karma it brings, have nevertheless opened centers in America, attracting, as Mahavir did, small groups of dedicated disciples. Jainism in the West has to be considerably changed—one cannot practice the scrupulously strict observance of nonviolence against creatures of the soil and the air, for example. But the disciples are likely to make yearly pilgrimages in groups to great Jain centers, such as the mystical Mount Abu in Rajasthan, and to practice Jainism as best they can at the feet of their masters, who not only teach yoga, meditation and vegetarian cooking but do so with the aid of video tapes. The new Jainism has to be an adaptation, perhaps for the better. But the central doctrine remains: the liberation of the individual. One of the leading Jain masters, the remarkable man known as Gurudev Chitrabhanu, tells his American disciples:

> Something in us knows that what we have is not permanent. For that we have to go beyond mental barriers and surrender to experience. It is surrendering to your own self. That awareness at the center of your being is always there, waiting to be your best friend, your highest self.

2

A PROPHETIC FAITH: THE ZOROASTRIANS

In 1754 a twenty-year-old Frenchman named Anquetil-Duperron came across four facsimile pages of an old Zoroastrian manuscript. About the middle of the eighteenth century, studies of this very ancient Iranian religion had become popular among European scholars, who were fascinated by the survival of the faith among a strange group of people in India called Parsees. The Prophet Zoroaster had long been known through the works of the classical Greeks, and later through the Arabs and the Persians. (This was a period when every scholar knew Arabic and Persian, as well as Greek and Latin and Hebrew.) Now, with the wholesale arrival of foreigners—English, French, Danes, Dutch and Portuguese—in India, many of the old writings of the different faiths in India were being examined.

Duperron decided to go to India to investigate the Parsees, who were concentrated mainly in a small city called Surat, some 150 miles north of the British bastion of Bombay. But travel to India was not lightly undertaken, for the British and the French were at war—the Seven Years War—and the fighting had spread from Europe to the New World, in Canada, and to the East, in India. Both nations were trying to gain the allegiances of the various native princes, the rajas, gaokars and nawabs, and to place their own men in the courts as advisers and even prime ministers. Duperron became a member of the French East India Company, the commercial venture that was devoted to trade and industry on the Indian subcontinent. He fought in the wars against the British—the French or their native allies were the invariable losers. In 1758, the year after the British inflicted a disastrous defeat on Indian allies of the French, Duperron was able to free himself of his company duties and to join the Parsees at Surat. Though short of funds and harassed by dysentery and fever, he stayed another three years, learning the languages and the religion. It was a long, hard task to persuade the reluctant priests to surrender parts of their precious, though not often used and little understood, copies of the old manuscripts. Four more years in solitary study passed before Duperron returned home with his trunkful of rare Zoroastrian documents. In 1771 he published the first complete translation in a European language of the Avesta, the primary Zoroastrian scripture.

THE AVESTA

The most sacred of all Zoroastrian writings, the Avesta has had a tragic history. Of the original work only the small part employed in the liturgy has survived. Zoroastrian tradition varies about the original work itself, one source stating that an archetypal copy was kept at the royal Persian library at Ishtakr, another tradition saying there were two copies, one at Persepolis, the other at Samarkand. Whether one or two copies, the manuscript itself was written on twelve thousand ox hides, in gold ink, and was destroyed by Alexander the Great in 330 B.C. However, a third of the text had been retained in the memories of the Zoroastrian priests, and this was written down. The work suffered further trials, which need not concern us. But whatever the Prophet left behind as doctrine was thus only partially retained.

The Avesta was written in a language called Zend. This created a great problem when Anquetil-Duperron released his translation and commentary to the scholarly world. A dispute broke out immediately, for many scholars rejected the authenticity of the Avesta, claiming that there was not only no other text of any kind in Zend (and some hinted that Duperron had even invented Zend for his own purposes), but that the work introduced concepts, gods, laws and regulations, folktales and wisdom which were unheard of, even through Greek and Arab sources. Critics also claimed it did a grave injustice to the celebrated simplicity, purity and wisdom of the great sage Zoroaster. Duperron sat out the storm of controversy. Once the disputes died down, scholars did further research, and the Avesta became a central focus of Oriental scholarship. Links were found between its primary language, Zend (it incorporated other languages as well), and Sanskrit, the tongue of the ancient Indians. Also, many of its themes and even the names of deities and spirits were found in the Hindus' oldest text, the Rig Veda. But despite all the scholarship, parts of the Avesta remain a puzzle, for there are many blanks in interpretation; the Zoroastrians of later years, not having a tradition of scholarship, did not understand the language of the original. Many mistakes were made in transcribing earlier documents; there were also erroneous commentaries and a disregard for the meaning of the original.

The surviving Avesta is about one tenth the length of the Bible. (However, somewhere along the way, a kind of encyclopedia, the Denkard, was drawn up, summarizing the contents of each of the twenty-one nasks, or chapters, of the original Avesta. The Denkard was written in Pahlavi, a Persian language.) Some parts of the Avesta are the work of the Prophet Zoroaster himself, or of his immediate disciples; these are written in an archaic form of Zend. Other sections are by later writers. The Zoroastrian portions, primarily a collection of songs or hymns, the Gathas, form the core of a section called the Yasna, which has many liturgical texts. The Gathas represent "pure" Zoroastrianism. Many of the later additions include material that diverges from the Prophet's own thinking, and may even be hostile to it. In all, it is a complex, interesting and troublesome work, of primary importance in the studies not only of Zoroastrianism but of early religious thought.

Duperron's scholarship meant a turning point in the lives of Zoroastrians. Here a disinterested foreigner had given shape and direction to their basic scriptures, had helped rescue works otherwise ignored or disregarded. Now the Parsees of India were able to revise their entire faith, to revive and renew it. Moreover, they were also able to help their coreligionists in Persia, who were living in a miserable state of oppression and poverty at the hands of the Muslims who ruled the nation.

And much of the West's ignorance of the Prophet himself was now dispelled. Europe was to learn something of the enigmatic but powerful figure of Zoroaster, and of his influence upon both Judaism and Christianity.

It has often been the fate of the Prophet to be ignored, especially in the Middle East. The ancient Jews furnish us with many excellent examples of this tragic fact: one lonely voice after another arose over the centuries to tell the people to reform, to abandon sinful ways, to look to the Lord, only to be ignored. And over and over again the people chose to listen to the false prophets, those who told them everything was fine, that life would go on in all its lush abandon, that they need not worry. And time after time the people found that not only had they fallen into sin, but that enemies had destroyed their towns, carried off their flocks, ravaged their women, even taken the people themselves into captivity.

The Prophet Zoroaster, that gnarled, crusty, outspoken Iranian who reformed the erring faith of his people in the sixth century B.C.—only to meet with hostility and rejection—stood squarely in the midst of the tradition. He restored the ancient beliefs falling into oblivion, reformed rites and rituals, and warned of the threat of evil and sin, yet few listened. Like most prophets, his message was not heard in his own time but in later ages, by people in other lands, of other races. *82-14269*

As in the case of his contemporary the great Jain leader Mahavir, who lived far to the south in the burning continent of India, Zoroaster's life is encrusted with much myth and legend. Hard facts are lost in a sea of romantic legendizing. Even the date of his birth is not only unclear but placed by his followers at an impossibly early time. The Zoroastrians have been rather emphatic in setting six thousand to seven thousand B.C. as the approximate period, according to several of their own historians. The Greek historians of the classical period, relying upon hearsay, are probably responsible for this error, which has been all too eagerly taken up by the faithful. Considering the primitive state of civilization at this time, the seventh millennium B.C. is hardly a likely possibility, for the Zoroastrian scriptures describe life in a royal court, and a type of society and ways of existence which were quite advanced; also, the language in which Zoroaster wrote probably had not been brought to Iran until some four thousand years later. So, pinpointing the most likely time, scholars have set a date for the Prophet's birth and death at 626–551 B.C., give or take a few years. This would place him only slightly earlier than Mahavir, the Lord Buddha and the great Chinese sages Lao-tzu and Confucius.

[33]

Where he was born is another question, though of lesser importance. He may have been born in a town called Rae, near the present Iranian city of Tehran, or in the vicinity of Lake Urumiah in Azerbaijan in the mountains of western Iran (again the town is called Rae), or at Rhages (or Rae) in Media, in central Iran. These are as near as one gets to the early facts about Zoroaster. What is important is his message, not the legends of his origins. Yet we must wade through at least some of these legends, for they are the very foundations of what the young Zoroastrian first learns about the Prophet, before the high doctrines are taught.

Zoroaster's childhood, like that of Mahavir, Buddha and, later, the Punjabi Saint Guru Nanak, is filled with mystical events. Without making judgments about their truth or accuracy, a few may be recounted. Zoroaster was much better known to the ancient Greeks and Romans, and much of what Zoroastrians publish today in their books comes from foreign sources, reabsorbed into their faith. In classical times Zoroaster was more famous in the West than Moses or King David, and the Greeks, with their passion for knowledge of all kinds, picked up much legend about him. According to one such legend, the Prophet's guardian angel entered into a hoama plant, which was consumed by a priest while he was enjoying the divine rites; at the same time "a ray of heaven's glory entered into the bosom of a maid of noble lineage; the priest married the maid and the imprisoned angel mingled with the imprisoned ray and Zoroaster took his earthly existence." This is the kind of cosmic-birth myth found in many religions. Buddha's was of the same order, except that in some versions a white elephant gave his mother a flower, this in a dream.

The Roman historian Pliny, who must have been working with second- or third-hand documents, or else heard the story from a traveler, wrote, "Zoroaster was the only human being who laughed at birth," all other babies presumably either crying or frowning.

Zoroaster's birth was not welcomed by certain forces of Evil. The Avesta states the "Soul of the World" had petitioned the Almighty God, Ahura Mazda, to send for "the appointment of a strong valiant hero who could crush the criminals with his superior might." Ahura Mazda sent not a warrior but "a holy gentle individual," Zoroaster, whose soul was still in paradise as an angelic being. Thus we see in Zoroastrian teaching that not only are there individual souls but that there is a paradise—two fundamental concepts of importance in the Western religions. It was the Prophet's mission on earth to proclaim the Truth and to triumph over Evil. In Zoroastrian belief both Truth and Evil work ultimately for Righteousness. Evil is created to test mankind but will be overcome.

Much folklore surrounds the figure of the young Zoroaster. Terrorists, aware of his reputation for sanctity even as a child, tried to murder him on several occasions, but a series of miracles saved his life. A fire into which he was thrown was extinguished without human interference; herds of horses and cattle did not trample upon him when he was placed in their path; wolves were unable to open their jaws in attacking him; an assassin's dagger was deflected, and so on.

There is no doubt that at the age of fifteen he retreated into a cave atop a mountain to spend a long period in meditation—ten years in some versions, fifteen in others. At the end of this period he experienced a heavenly vision of Ahura Mazda, the Supreme Lord. "I acknowledge Thee as wholly beneficent, O Wise Lord," he chanted in his meditative poems, the Yasnas, which he wrote during this time. He received the divine message of Purity, Uprighteousness and Truth, the three standards of Zoroastrian conduct.

Returning to the world, he began to preach that "Righteousness is the best good." He was attempting not to found a new religion but to purify the old one, Mazdayasni, "the religion of Mazda," the Omniscient and Supreme Lord, into which he had

[35]

been born, and to reestablish it as the true faith over the Daevayasni, the religion of the Devil as a mighty destroyer, which had become powerful in recent centuries. His mission to restate the ancient doctrines and to assert the preeminence of the One True God met with stiff opposition and even persecution, for he was preaching in a time of social chaos, when the old settled pastoral communities were threatened by marauding nomadic tribal societies which plundered and murdered.

The Prophet wandered through Iran, Afghanistan and Turanistan without gaining much of a hearing, passing ten years on the road in the life of the holy nomad. (Some of the locales mentioned in the Avesta can still be identified.) During this period, the Prophet experienced visions, seven in all, which showed him the mysteries of heaven. From various divine beings, angels and personified abstractions he received commands and injunctions to pass on to mankind. He was told of the doctrine of the purity of the body—Zoroastrians are extremely concerned about cleanliness—and of the soul—there is much positive emphasis on what one must do, and little on what one must not do. He was especially enjoined to care for animals, particularly the cow and the dog, both of which play important roles in Zoroastrian life. The messages emphasized the necessity of keeping the earth, water and fire undefiled, and fire in particular was to be a key tool in Zoroastrian ritual. One of the important tenets was that of civil reform. Another included the universal obligation to speak the truth and not to lie. His ecstatic experiences included a revelation of the future, which included the resurrection of the dead and the afterlife. But even during these excursions into the heavens, he was warned of a spiritual enemy, Angra Mainyu, or Ahriman, the Devil. From the dazzling splendor of the supernatural he caught a glimpse of the darkness, filth, stench and torment of the Worst World.

With this he was tempted by the Devil himself, who sought

unsuccessfully to persuade Zoroaster to renounce the True Religion of Mazda.

In his preaching to the people as he wandered, Zoroaster divided the world into two basic groups: the followers of Truth and the followers of the Lie, led by the two spirits, Asha and Druj, which share the universe between them. Good and Evil, God and the Devil, are in constant warfare with each other. How is the conflict to be resolved? Man is a free agent, Zoroaster taught, and he is to solve the problem by electing right and choosing goodness, as the Prophet himself was doing. The reward will be eternal joys at the resurrection, "when the dead shall rise up, the quick be made mortal and the world, as desired, made perfect."

But, as we know about the words of prophets, Zoroaster's fell upon deaf ears. During his initial period of preaching he made but a single convert, a cousin. Then he was called by King Vishtaspa, the chief of the Chrosmian confederacy, a group of powerful tribal chiefs. Vishtaspa asked to hear the tenets of the Prophet's beliefs, but then demanded physical proof. Among other miracles, the Prophet displayed heavenly fire, which could not be extinguished by the court magicians, but which would not burn anyone who touched it. Vishtaspa accepted Zoroaster as the prophet of Ahura Mazda and gave him a house. But the court magicians were determined to get rid of Zoroaster. They placed the tools of magic—hair, human bones, the heads of animals, excreta and other matter used in casting spells—under his bed. Zoroaster was put in prison. Then, upon curing the king's horse after the magicians had failed, he was released and restored to power. The animal's legs had been withdrawn into its body; the prophet released each leg upon the promise of the king and queen and the royal children to follow his teachings.

The king now spread the revived faith of Ahura Mazda, and built fire temples for its proper celebration.

Zoroaster's death occurred during the wars which arose partly as the result of his teachings. Many of the people of Iran rejected his reforms, preferring their own worship of various demons, nature deities and gods of abstract qualities (such as knowledge, speech and love), and practiced the ritual slaughter of animals, especially of cows and bulls. During a war with a Turkish tribe known as Turanians, the Prophet was attacked from behind by an enemy soldier while praying at a fire temple. As he fell he cast his prayer beads at his assailant, who dropped dead. This is an interesting incident, for normally the great saint or prophet forgives his enemies, even those who have mortally wounded him.

In Zoroastrian teaching, the Prophet cast aside his physical body when his work was completed in order to return to the Lord, whose messenger he was. There will be another prophet. Although Zoroaster was married (he is said to have had three sons and three daughters), he did not select one of his own children as a successor, nor will he return himself. His successor and eventual messiah is the curious figure of Prince Peshotan. The prince was so holy that he attained immortality during his lifetime. Some of the latter Zoroastrian texts refer to him as the future prophet of Iran. He has fifty-one (in some versions 151) disciples, with whom he lives in a cave monastery on sacred Mount Alburz. At the proper time he will return to save the world. His cult seems to be the basis of the development of the doctrine of the Hidden Imam among Iranian Muslims of the Shi'a sect, who also believe that a savior, now living secretly in their country, will someday appear in public for the benefit of all mankind, saving the righteous and destroying the wicked.

The Prophet's teachings had more success after his death than during his lifetime. Various Persian emperors extended Iranian rule farther and farther, by the twin policies of war and marriage. Cyrus the Great and his son Cambyses finally built one great empire, which extended from India to the Aegean Sea, and

The Prophet Zoroaster displays the sacred fire which does not burn to the Emperor Vishtaspa, who had asked for proof of the prophet's powers. Surrounding the emperor are the court magicians, who later tried to have the Prophet banished.

included parts of Egypt, Libya and Ethiopia. It was Cyrus who freed the Jews in Babylon in 606 B.C. by defeating Nebuchadnezzar, returning to them their sacred vessels of gold and silver and contributing to the cost of rebuilding the Temple of Jerusalem. The Book of Isaiah speaks of Cyrus as "the Anointed of the Lord" and the "shepherd" who performs the Lord's pleasure. But it was more than freedom that the Jews carried away from Babylon, for they also brought with them certain of the Mazdayani beliefs, which would eventually work themselves into Christianity, as well as into various sects, such as the Manichaeans, later considered heretical.

Greeks under Alexander the Great took over the empire in the fourth century B.C., and they were followed in later centuries by various Persian dynasties. The Sassanians made Zoroastrianism the state religion, but by this time it had been seriously corrupted, the Prophet's pure monotheism being infiltrated with doctrines which turned it into a complicated system of rituals and scholastics, with much magic and superstition. Zoroastrianism had become scrupulously formal. The priesthood gained unlimited power and prestige. The ruling classes, no longer the outgoing warriors who had made the empire great, now spent their lives in ease and intrigue in the luxuries of the court.

By A.D. 635 the empire was dying — in its last four years it had eleven rulers, two of them women — when the Arabs, converted to Islam only eighty years earlier, swept over it like a great storm. The common people took to Islam quickly, but it was a curious form of the faith, for certain of the tenets of the old religion, including some of the superstitions, survived. Also, many small pockets of Zoroastrians, primarily in the province of Fars, held on to their beliefs. Today there still is a small group, estimated at some twenty thousand, centered on the town of Yazd, who follow the religion of Ahura Mazda. But many Zoroastrians chose to emigrate rather than submit to the Muslims. Some went to

China, others to India. In both countries there were already established colonies of traders who were Zoroastrians. Those in China flourished for many centuries—there were reports of Zoroastrian fire altars there as late as A.D. 905—but eventually they were absorbed into the general populace and disappeared into history.

When those Zoroastrians who came to be known as Parsees (that is, Persians) arrived in India is not known, and perhaps never will be. Zoroastrian merchants had probably come to India as early as the third century B.C. The mass of refugees arrived at dates set from 636 to 936. One Parsee tradition establishes the arrival of a group at Sanjan, on India's west coast, in 716. For their safe-being, the local raja imposed the condition that they never attempt to make converts, a condition they have observed faithfully ever since. (Even the child of a mixed marriage will not be received as a Parsee.) A second major group of Zoroastrians came to India during Timur's invasion of Persia in the fourteenth century.

From the very beginning Parsees progressed rapidly, being engaged in agriculture, weaving, shipbuilding, carpentry, coastal trade and general business, and in all crafts except those which had to do with fire (such as blacksmithing), for fire was sacred and could be handled only by the priests. When the British began their exploitation of India, the major Parsee center shifted from Sanjan to Surat (it was here that Anquetil-Duperron began his studies). As merchants the Parsees could not help becoming involved with the British East India Company, which, rather than the Crown, represented British interests in India. When the British made Bombay the center of trade, the Parsees followed. Today they are a small but prosperous community of some 120,000 people, highly educated, intelligent, philanthropic and socially conscious, occupying a beneficial role in India far beyond their limited numbers.

ZOROASTRIANISM

Zoroastrianism, the religion of the ancient Iranians and of the Parsees and the remnant in Yazd, is a complex faith and often not well understood, either by the faithful themselves or by the many Western scholars who have attempted to unravel its profundities. The faithful tend to leave the complexities to the priests but carefully follow the prescribed prayers and rituals, and observe the celebrations. They pay special attention to the ethical and social teachings of the Prophet. How great the priests' own understanding is, is a mystery, for true scholars among them are rare, and much of the doctrine is quite esoteric, its origins, development and interpretation having been lost in antiquity. In Iran some Islamic influence has been noted, and the Parsees in India have been affected not only by Hinduism and Islam but by Christianity as well.

Western scholars, who have been fascinated by Zoroastrianism, often tend to interpret in terms of their own beliefs. What is bad is that they have become involved in minutiae of translation, so that scholars' academic quarrels over words, or a letter or an accent, replace attempts at interpretation and proper translation. One can plow through volumes of dense academic prose dealing with Western views of the Zoroastrians without finding the simplest idea of what a Parsee believes or how he or she worships.

A major problem for the scholars — and for the faithful — is that the ancient texts not only are incomplete and fragmented but confusing, poorly copied in the past and difficult to translate. Yet among the Zoroastrians there is a fairly clear idea of the faith and how one practices it.

The Prophet is a divinely appointed teacher, thoroughly human and real, who suffered at the hands of Evil, a power which, like Good or Truth, is created by Ahura Mazda, the Omniscient

On the Parsee New Year, the entryways to houses are decorated with chalk drawings to mark the festival of Nowroz Pateti. The date is the spring equinox (March 21), and the swastika is a sun symbol. On Nowroz Pateti the faithful put on new clothing, forgive offenses of others, and attend a fire temple.

Lord. Both forces work ultimately for Righteousness, as the Prophet taught. And it was his mission to triumph over Evil through Righteousness. Zoroaster, like all mankind, had a free choice; he, like anyone else, was at liberty to choose one or the other. But Righteousness is always, must be, the only choice.

Zoroastrianism itself is an exceedingly complex faith, and the average layman is hard put to explain the details in full, though most Zoroastrians, especially the Parsees, know more of their religion than those of other faiths do of theirs. Like most peoples, they believe that there was a time before Creation. Then God, or Ahura Mazda, existed in a state of dormancy—formless, timeless and motionless. This was the period of Boundless Time, eternity without beginning and without end. This preexistence was God's absolute aspect.

Then the Divine Will moved and spoke. Limited Time evolved from the placid ocean of eternity. With His Will at the center, God remained the One, the Omniscient Source of Existence—or Ahura Mazda. The Prophet called this aspect "God without a predecessor." But the One became two, spirit and matter, life and form. Critics call this a "duality," implying contradiction and strife, but the Zoroastrians state that, rather, the two modes should be thought of as a polarity, for the universe develops along two lines, Spen, or increase, and Angra, or decrease. The real aspects of both are invisible; they are known as mino, or mental concepts. Angra-mino was formalized as Satan, and mankind was asked to discriminate between Good and Evil.

The Zoroastrians have been plagued by a returning question: How could Evil come from Ahura Mazda, the embodiment of Good and of Righteousness? But they see Evil as only relative, depending on the observer's point of view. Whatever thwarts the growth of the soul, whatever is against the will of God, is evil.

Unlike the All-Powerful Deity of the Judeo-Christian faiths, Ahura Mazda, God, acts for administrative purposes through a great bureaucracy. (There are echoes of this in descriptions of angels as messengers throughout the Bible and in some descriptions of heavenly choirs in the Apocalyptic books of the New Testament.) Ahura Mazda has two great subordinates, Ahu (Ruler) and Ratu (Teacher), who govern the temporal and spiritual spheres, respectively. They are the Will and the Wisdom aspect of God or Law and Grace.

Ahura Mazda Himself shows three aspects: Ahura, the Creator; Volumnan, the Preserver; and Asha Vahista, the Reconstructor. These aspects have parallels in the Hindu triad of Brahma, the Creator; Vishnu, the Preserver; and Shiva, who destroys in order for Creation to commence again. But there is a Judeo-Christian connection also, for the three hold joint consultations over the appointment of a Savior. In an Avestan hymn written by the Prophet, Ahura Mazda says, "I am the Creator, the Preserving Nourisher and the Smiter."

Below the various ranks of heavenly administrators — there are thirty major angels, for each day of the month, and many more for other areas — there are the sevenfold aspects of the archangels, who dominate the seven kingdoms and creatures of nature — men, animals, fire and the heavenly bodies, the mineral kingdom, the earth, the waters and the vegetable kingdom. These archangels are "united in thought, word and deed," and possess "power, intelligence and love" derived from the "One without a Second." Beyond these groups there are numerous others, for each heavenly body has its own invisible spiritual guardian. The living and the dead, too, have guardian angels. Innumerable divine sparks enliven and ensoul every atom and every cell, for Ahura Mazda is Immanent, and there is no corporeal existence without its indwelling spiritual force. But despite the multiplicity of divine sparks, from archangel down to the most minute celestial being, the Zoroastrians consider themselves monotheists. The heavenly hierarchy exists to aid in the running of the universe.

The Entities, as they are called, are parts of the One Source.

Each person has a soul—the Zoroastrian term is "fravashi." Until the soul discovers the right path of reunion with God, it wanders in deceit and destruction. One is free to sin, but sin is "a corrosive and consuming influence." All evil thoughts, words and deeds are due to a lack of intelligence. A sinful person is temporarily insane, and a criminal is a child-soul. A Zoroastrian must constantly review his own conduct so as to weigh all causes and effects. Then, if one has erred, one must return to the right path.

Thus, possessing an immortal soul, man is composed of matter and spirit. But there are two forms of spirit—a vital breath, which is a faculty of discernment, a conscience—its creation preceding the body's—and the fravashi, a kind of external soul, also preexistent. Only the fravashi has life after death.

The concept of the afterlife is expressed in the Avesta. The fravashi will go to heaven, hell or an intermediate domain. Man will be judged on what he or she has accomplished according to his or her own free will. In the end, the body will be resurrected and united with the soul. Only the good will survive, for all evil will be destroyed. And in the afterworld each individual will live in family groups in his or her original perfected form, exempt from all sin and enjoying eternal bliss. In his life the Zoroastrian attempts to put these general themes of Zoroastrian theology into actual practice.

THE ZOROASTRIAN'S LIFE

Daily life is structured for a positive appreciation of Ahura Mazda and his creation. The Zoroastrian must pray five times a day, beginning at dawn. The day is divided into "gehs" (the word means watch). The first runs until noon; the second—"the period of heat"—until 3:00 P. M.; "the period of turning out" runs until sunset; sunset until midnight is the time for the recital of hymns and epics; lastly, the time until sunrise is known as "drawing near to dawn." Everyone who has been formally received into the Zoroastrian community is obligated to pray. One faces the sun while praying. The prayers change slightly during the day and at different seasons.

Each geh has its own protector archangel. In its esoteric significance the geh is the symbol of the spiritual evolution of the soul in its ascent to liberation, light and wisdom — an ascent commencing with dawn, the shattering of darkness by the light of the sun, the heavenly fire which is the symbol of Ahura Mazda and his own "son."

The sun, and fire in all its forms, play primary roles in Zoroastrianism. Fire is the representative of God, not only His most important creation but also His physical manifestation. The sun as a form of fire is "the most beautiful body of God." Fire is bright, always points upward, is always pure. The temples which contain fire are the centers of worship, and they may be magnificent buildings, such as those built by the Parsees in the nineteenth century under the influence of English colonial architecture. There are three classes of fire temple. The highest, dedicated to the angel of victory, contains a fire ignited from seventeen different sources, including fire from lightning, fire from a baker's oven, and even from a cremation ground, a place that the Zoroastrians normally consider degrading, for, unlike the Hindus, they do not burn their dead but expose them to the vultures. The other two classes are consecrated with fewer forms of fire. All fire temples are prohibited to non-Zoroastrians, and even the faithful may not enter certain parts of the temples. Marriages, the initiation of the young into the faith, the consecration of priests and other ceremonies usually are celebrated at a fire temple.

One becomes a full member of the community in a ceremony the Parsees call navzote; in Iran it is known as nozad. Either term means, roughly, new worshiper, or new birth. One undergoes the ceremony between the ages of seven and fifteen, and it is binding upon both boys and girls. It is a joyous occasion, with relatives and friends present as the young Zoroastrian says the creed. As the newcomer enters the hall (or the event may be held at home), a priest waves a coconut, rice, a pot of water, egg or some other item of food over his or her head. This is to remove undesirable emanations and to purify the etheric aura. After ritual prayers, the sudreh, the spotless white shirt emblematic of the Zoroastrian faith, and the kusti, the wool cord, are bestowed.

Navzote, and the sudreh and kusti, are good examples of how the Zoroastrians endow a simple ceremony and two simple objects — a shirt and a cord belt — with esoteric meanings of such poetic and mystical depth that one is always reminded of his relationship with the Supreme and His world. The sudreh is a symbol of faith in Ahura Mazda. The shirt, which is made up of patches of cloth (to signify poverty) is worn next to the skin; ordinary clothing may be worn over it. The sudreh is "the garment of the good mind," the outward sign of inward grace and the armor against Satan. A small pocket on the front has a dual importance: it reminds the Zoroastrian that his faith should be a source of encouragement, and it is a pocket in which to collect (symbolically, of course) good deeds. This is to remind the individual that when he stands before God at the Last Judgment his pocket must be filled with the fruits of meritorious acts on behalf of others. One places his right hand in the pocket when praying; and when a Zoroastrian wants to assure someone of his sincerity, he places his hand in the pocket.

The kusti is made of seventy-two threads of lamb's wool, symbolic of the seventy-two chapters of the Yasna, a section of the Avesta. It is the "sword-belt" of the righteous in the battle against evil. The kusti is looped three times around the waist and is tied in four knots, two in front, two behind. The loops signify the three aspects of Ahura Mazda as Creator, Preserver and Reconstructor. The knots remind the individual of the four daily duties: worship of God in self-sacrifice, loyal obedience to the teachings of the Prophet, constant struggle against Satan and absolute confidence in God's laws and decrees. Zoroastrian works multiply the symbolism indefinitely, but one more meaning must be included here, which involves the navzote ceremony. Here the kusti symbolizes a rope whereby the new member of the community descends "into the vault of his higher nature, to rediscover God's mysteries," knowledge of which he had lost when his soul had "fallen into the flesh" — that is, when it was born in a human body. This "retirement into a cave" to seek wisdom reminds one of the Prophet Zoroaster's fifteen-year retreat in the wilds of Mount Alburz when he was having his heavenly dialogue with Ahura Mazda, the Supreme Lord.

3

THE SIKHS

In the fifteenth century India was a scene of gory religious tensions and fratricidal wars between rival kingdoms and faiths—Lodhi kings, the Rajputs, various Afghans, Persians and Turks, and the Moguls, as well as between ordinary Hindus and Muslims. The people were heavily taxed by whatever powers were in control—the chauthth, or one quarter, was normal, but some despots might add on another fifty percent.

Most of the upheaval took place on the vast northern plain that is formed by two river sytems. On the west, running from the foothills of Afghanistan and Baluchistan, is the Punjab, the land of the five rivers, all of which drop down from the Himalayas, that great range of the world's tallest mountains which cut off most of the Indian subcontinent from Asia itself. East of the Punjab is the wide plain created by the Ganges, which is joined by other rivers as it crosses eastward to culminate in the crowded delta that forms Bengal and Bangladesh.

The Punjab is one of the most fertile areas in all the world, a farmland of a richness that equals any in Russia, Europe or the Americas. Its rivers water it well, and since primordial times have attracted settlers who have built villages, towns and even cities along the leisurely streams. But like a great sea, the Punjab is open and vulnerable to enemies. Battles more like naval encounters than land wars have raged across its flatlands since the earliest known times. But not only armies were free to cross the Punjab: so did ideas, as well as trade. From the evidence found in the early Punjab cities it is known that it was the seat of Hinduism, primordial examples some five thousand years old having been found. Later many of its people became Buddhists, for, as easily as armies and caravans, the teachings of the Lord Buddha crossed the Punjab and traveled up into Afghanistan through the same passes that served invaders from the north.

In the eighth century Arab armies, in their whirlwind conquest of the known world, brought with them Islam, that great monotheistic faith which taught the brotherhood of all mankind, without regard for color or caste, in submission to Allah, God Himself. The Buddhists virtually disappeared—slaughtered or converted. With the Punjab's Hindus there were slightly different results: many of the Hindus at the bottom of the social and caste systems embraced Islam, with its egalitarian beliefs and its doctrine of salvation now—in this life—rather than at the end of a wearying series of rebirths, as Hinduism taught. But many Hindu rajas refused to submit. The wars were endless, as new waves of Muslims of different origins—Turks, Persians, Afghans—followed. The foreign armies devastated and impoverished large areas. The local rajas and sultans (for not even Muslims themselves were exempt from the attacks) were murdered or robbed of their treasures, Hindu temples were looted and destroyed, large numbers of people were massacred, and slaves, artisans and craftsmen were taken to Persia and Afghanistan.

[51]

Yet there were some positive movements. Perhaps because of the intolerable religious and social conditions, there was much creative work in all fields—architecture, painting, music and philosophy. Some of the greatest of all Indian religious poetry dates from this period, the fifteenth and sixteenth centuries. Also, as part of this widespread creative activity, popular devotional and mystical movements had taken a powerful form. Numerous wandering holy men, of undisputed sanctity, both Hindu and Muslim, were walking about the countryside, singing their mystical poems and attracting great numbers of followers with their doctrines of devotion—rather than rites and ceremonies—as the way to God. It was in such a time of turmoil and of mass mystical movements that the founder of the Sikhs, Guru Nanak, was born.

On the night of the full moon, in the month of November, A.D. 1469, a boy was born into the family of Kalu, a Hindu farmer in the Punjab in western India. The child was named Nanak, in honor of his older sister, Bini Nanaki. The family bore the surname Bedi, actually a kind of title, signifying that they were descended from ancient kings of the lunar race, exemplified by the legendary ruler Ramchandra. Thus the family, as descendants of kings, were kshatriyas, members of the Hindu warrior caste, and were well off. Nanak's birthplace is Talwindi, now on the Pakistani side of the Punjab, which was divided during the partition of India in 1947. The town's population was a mixture of Muslims and Hindus. Nanak's father, though a Hindu, was an official in the court of the local sultan, a Rajput prince called Rai Bular. At the age of five, young Nanak was sent to the local school, run by the village Brahmin, or priest.

From his earliest years Nanak had been noted as a withdrawn child, contemplative and fond of religious company, especially the wandering holy men, the Hindu yogis and sadhus, and the Muslim

[52]

faquirs and pirs who passed through Talwindi. In his first day at school his mind was obviously not on his lesson, an attempt by the Brahmin to teach him the alphabet.

"Why aren't you writing?" demanded the teacher.

"I was thinking not of the 'A' but of 'Soi,'" said Nanak.

The Brahmin wanted to know what Nanak meant by "Soi."

"It is the sound of the Creative," said Nanak quietly.

"How can you talk about Creation when you are an ignorant child?"

"Because there can be no beginning without the eternal sound of creativity having been learned," said Nanak.

The Brahmin, who had been inclined to thump the child over the head with a stick, realized that he was dealing with someone unusual. In fact, the old accounts say, the teacher was "awakened." He brought Nanak home to Mehta Kalu, and said, "Your son is beyond my teaching. He knows all that is to be known." He added, "You are truly blessed in the birth of an avatar as son to you." An avatar is an incarnation of God Himself. But the father thought the Brahmin was being sarcastic.

Nanak's education continued at home, where he was taught the subjects necessary for survival and advancement at the time — bookkeeping, Sanskrit and Persian, the latter the language of the conquerors. He also learned the customs of the warrior caste of which he was a member, and he gained a vast insight into the various systems of Indian philosophy, thought and mysticism, including yoga, and of the principles of orthodox Islam and of Sufism, its mystical counterpart.

As a budding saint, Nanak exhibited the hallmarks of mysticism, of the types that in retrospect seem interesting but can be annoying for the people who have to suffer the mystic's eccentricities. As a child he refused to accept the white thread which was a mark of his caste. In a poem he wrote about that time expressing his religious beliefs, he stated that the cotton threads ritually worn by Hindus of the three highest castes were worthless, that the only true thread was the Thread of Truth woven out of the essence of Love Divine.

Young Nanak showed nothing but signs of uselessness. He was put out to herd the family cattle. After a few days at this boring task he went into a mystical trance, while the cattle wandered off to graze in a neighbor's fields. Nanak was lost for hours in contemplation of the Divine Form, the One and the Only One. Finally the neighboring farmer, furious over the destruction of his pasturage, shook Nanak out of his ecstatic trance. Nanak said, "Dear one, the yield from the field this time will be more abundant than ever before. The happiness of the cattle will bring the blessings of prosperity to you." The farmer complained to the police, who came to inspect the damage. But as Nanak had said—and as one expects from the accounts of the lives of holy men—the farmer's fields grew lusher than before.

On another occasion, again while supposedly tending his family's herds, Nanak fell asleep at noonday in the blistering Indian sun. A cobra (a sacred creature), sensing the divine in young Nanak, "crawled near the head of young Nanak," writes one of the saint's biographers, "and spread the umbrella of its hood, thus protecting the head and the face, on which it had seen the halo of light celestial."

Rai Bular, the local governor, witnessed the scene and was impressed by the young boy's signs of being an advanced soul. But while others might see the saint in Nanak, his father thought of him as nothing but a problem adolescent. Obviously Nanak was a failure as a herdsman. Now Mehta Kalu tried to make his son take over a piece of family land as a farm.

"Son," he said, "you may be dreaming of the riches of the other world and rejecting this one. But don't forget, those who do not gain wealth here remain poor and needy and they pass on as paupers to the other world. So, become a farmer and be prosperous. No longer will trances help you, especially when I am gone."

Listening patiently to the well-meant fatherly advice, young Nanak finally replied, "Dear Father, I am already farming, devotedly and diligently. Please believe me that what I am doing is true farming."

Irritated, the father snapped, "What farming, and where are your earnings?"

The answer comes in a poem, translated by one of Nanak's descendants:

> My body is the farm
> and inner light,
> The ploughing farmer,
> I level the ups and downs
> of the clods and the lumps
> with the plough of contentment,
> And I thrash the field of the self
> with the flail of humility.
> It is in this field,
> dear father,
> that the blooms of love sprout.
> Seated in the certainty of truth
> I watch the crop grow
> and daily earn my wages
> in the rupees of ecstasy.

So, Nanak will not farm. In retrospect one wonders at the patience of the father, for this was an age when the patriarch of a family ruled with an iron hand, and the normal father would have beaten his son into obedience. The father suggests keeping a shop as a means of earning a living. Another poem comes by way of answer:

> The frailty of the physique,
> the body brittle
> are the shop.

[55]

Inside this shop
I make contemplation
the container.
In that container
I stock the grain of
the Name Divine,
the truest of true commodities.
So, Truth, dear father,
is the wealth I earn
from the shop
of the self.

Still another idea is offered by the father, bringing yet another poetic reply. The father wants Nanak to become a horse trader.

Only he who breeds
the horses of truth
is the true dealer.

And so on, for, as Nanak points out, everyone must sooner or later go to the other world, where "the true dealer shall reside eternally, lodged in the abode of bliss."

And what about government service? the father wonders. Again Nanak offers a poem.

The only Master I serve
is Him and none else . . .
With the grace of His name
I live in the glory of surrender
to the Great Master
whose one look
of favor
confers Bliss unimaginable
as the reward for serving Him.

"Uttering these words of light, the Sat Guru [Nanak] passed

into an ecstatic state of self-forgetful trance," adds his descendant, B. P. L. Bedi.

Coming out of the trance, Nanak went to his room. Soon his mother came to reason with him. I need not add in full the poem that her entreaties brought forth, though Nanak said some lines which were virtually heretical for a high-caste Hindu to utter:

> It is only praising Him
> that makes one high-born
> and forgetting Him
> makes men low-born.
> Caste or birth does not
> make men high or low.

These last few lines were to become one of his central teachings, that neither caste nor the accidents of good birth makes one any better than anyone else.

The parents call in a doctor. Nanak tells him to look within and observe the pulse of the inner self. Nanak is not ill, but is "suffering from the pain of separation from Him." Nanak adds, "Suffering from such a pain is the real sign of human well-being and sound health." Like the sultan, the doctor realizes that Nanak is someone unusual. He inquires about the form of the suffering.

"The pain of separation clothes you with bliss Divine and the waves of joy transform the dross of the self, like an alchemist's workshop, into the golden purity of inner light."

The doctor tells Kalu and his wife, Matta Rai, that their son is the messenger of God and leaves.

The father at last finds a task to which Nanak agrees. Giving his son twenty rupees (roughly the equivalent in purchasing power of twenty dollars), the father sends the boy to the bazaar in town to buy whatever can be sold at a profit in the villages. Nanak goes, accompanied by his childhood companion, Bala, also a Hindu. On the way the two boys meet a group of sadhus, holy men, who claim they are hungry. Needless to say, Nanak buys food for them with the twenty rupees. Explaining later to Mehta Kalu, Nanak says that the profit from the trip came not from buying and selling but in "the goods of good deeds, the profit of bliss-conferring merit." He adds, "I have traded in Truth." The incidents multiply, and make edifying stories for later generations of the faithful, for this emphasis on the uselessness of the ordinary world is a constant theme in Nanak's life, and in those of his followers, the Sikhs, as they were later called.

Somehow the parents succeeded in marrying Nanak to a girl from another kshatriya family — such marriages were and usually are even now arranged by the clan. He had two sons, Sri Chand and Laksmidas, who took minor roles in the background of the saintly parent's glory. Sri Chand, the older, lived to be a hundred and forty-nine, having founded the Udasee sects of the Sikhs, a group of homeless, wandering dervishlike recluses. Laksmidas remained a householder and continued the line of the family name, the house of the moon, the revered Bedis.

Through his sister, who had married a minister of the governor's court in the major town of Sultanpur, Nanak, now seventeen, was given a job as a clerk in the government offices. For three years he lived peacefully with his new wife and his newly born sons. Then a famine broke out, and as might be expected, Nanak opened the government warehouses to the starving. The stocks of grain were apparently depleted. Nanak had not kept the accounts properly, and an investigation was ordered. However, when the granary doors were opened, the warehouses were full, and the cash boxes were crammed with money. His reputation having been vindicated, Nanak walked away, not only from government service but from the worldly life itself. He announced that having lived as a householder, his mission was now to teach other householders how to live as true human beings while leading normal domestic lives, to know God and be godly in daily life as fathers and mothers, sons and daughters. And off he went to seek final enlightenment.

I give these examples of Nanak's early life because they follow a kind of pattern shared by many great religious figures. We have seen remarkable similarities in the lives of the Jain Mahavir and the Prophet Zoroaster. On the Indian subcontinent, the Lord Buddha also led the same kind of life as a young man, though in his case the legends reach far more fantastic proportions than those of the others, the hard facts being difficult to winnow from the great mass of legends that have accumulated over the twenty-six centuries since he lived — the known manuscripts alone total more pages (in more languages) than a single person could read in his entire life. Nanak's life, much closer to ours, is far more factual. Virtually everything he did or said was written down and commented upon by two close disciples, his childhood friend Bala and the Muslim saint Mardana, who accompanied Nanak and Bala on their wanderings. We might wish they had been more objective, less fanciful and not so given to embellishing interesting incidents with a veneer of unnecessary piety, but at least one can sense, if not see, the underlying truths in many cases.

Besides the childhood yearning for union with the Absolute shared by Mahavir (and Parsva, too, of course), Zoroaster, Buddha and Nanak, there is also a common background. All four (or five) individuals were members of the kshatriya, or warrior caste — the men who ruled — rather than of the priestly, higher caste. All lived in times of social upheaval, and all taught egalitarian doctrines, partly in response to the crushing powers of the clergy but partly because they had a sincere desire to open the path of salvation to everyone, not just the favored few, who comprised the clergy. What was important, considering the restrictions of the ages in which they lived and taught was that all, to some degree or other, broke down the barriers, at least partially, that otherwise prevented women from sharing in the Way to the Supreme. That many of the egalitarian doctrines were later subverted by their followers is not the fault of the originators of the various paths, but is due to the failure of the disciples to adhere more closely to the basic teachings.

Now, like his predecessors, Nanak began his search to break the earthly ties that bound him and to enter directly into union with his God.

Outside of Sultanpur, Nanak found a great tree on the banks of the Bayen River. Here he sat down in contemplation and passed into the Trance of Wonder. In such times of testing, the holy ones seem to go through identical situations: there are spirits — Furies or others — which attempt to stike fear into the saint's heart. Then beautiful women — in Nanak's case, the "Maidens of Mara" — offer sensual temptations and inducements. The final test — which may involve hundreds of temptations and last for days — is the offer of the crown of the entire world as a price for abandoning the spiritual life and returning to mundane affairs. Like other holy men who pass the test, Nanak overcame the Furies, rejected the heavenly maidens and refused the emperorship of the globe. He then passed into the Trance of Praise, his heart aglow with an inner light and inner sound of joy. For three nights and three days he remained in the ecstasy of the Trance Divine, communing with the Highest Lord. As he awoke from his ecstasy, a stream of praise flowed from his heart. The words he sang, the brief hymn that sprang forward spontaneously, is the basic utterance of the Sikh creed and is said aloud or silently upon all possible occasions. It is known as the Jap-ji, and forms also the opening passage of the Granth Saheb, the Sikh scriptures assembled later by Arjun Dev, the fifth Sikh Guru. I will give it in the original Punjabi, though few readers will be able to understand it, and then in English translation.

[60]

Ek Onkar sat nam, karta purkha.
Nirbhau nirvair.
Akal Moorat.
Ajooni, sehbhang.
Gur prasad.
Jap
Aad sach, jugaad sach.
Hae bhi sach.
Nanak, hosi bhi sach.

The Punjabi compresses much into the simple words—each has layers of meaning and depth to the initiate—and often translations are printed in the form below. Unfortunately, due to the complexity of the original, and the meanings each word has to the faithful, translations often read as if they were based upon different, unrelated texts. However, the translation by Nanak's direct descendant, B. P. L. Bedi, is as good and as concise as any, so I will quote it.

Ek	The one
Onkar	the parent of Sound creative
sat nam	Truth is your name
karta purkha.	Creator of existence and Lord of non-existence
Nirbhau	Of beginningless Beginning and Endless Ending
nirvair.	without an opposite.
Akal Moorat.	The embodiment of Immortality
Ajooni.	Free from the cycle of birth and death.
sehbhang	Self-manifested
Gur prasad.	Self-revealed, by grace of Himself
Jap	Praise the One
Aad sach	From beginningless beginning, truth is your name
jugaad sach	From the beginning of time, truth is your Name
Hae bhi sach	Even today, truth is your name
Nanak	Nanak says,
hosi bhi sach	Even to the Endless end of time, truth shall be your name.

Trilochan Singh, another Sikh, translates it differently:

> There is one God,
> Eternal Truth is His Name;
> Maker of all things,
> Fearing nothing and at enmity with nothing,
> Timeless is His Image;
> Not begotten, being of His own Being:
> By the grace of the Guru, made known to men.
> JAP: THE MEDITATION
> AS HE WAS IN THE BEGINNING: THE TRUTH,
> SO THROUGHOUT THE AGES,
> HE EVER HAS BEEN: THE TRUTH,
> SO EVEN NOW HE IS TRUTH IMMANENT,
> SO FOR EVER AND EVER HE SHALL BE
>   TRUTH ETERNAL.

I could quote translations until one longs for death and rebirth—freedom from the endless round of translations—but the preceding will suffice.

The three nights and three days on the river bank mark a transition point in Nanak's life. In a literal sense, he had been reborn a second time, or a third, for the Hindu of the higher castes experiences two births, that of his natural birth and that when he is given the sacred thread to be reborn a member of his caste. With this new birth Nanak ceased to be a caste Hindu and became instead a member of the wandering mystical horde, rootless and footloose, and bound to nothing but his devotion to the Supreme Lord. Now he was constantly on the move, visiting various holy men and holy places. On most of his travels he was accompanied by his old friends Bala and the Muslim mystic Mardana, who is noted for his playing of a stringed instrument called the rubab (in some translations it is referred to as a rebeck).

With his companions Nanak wandered as far west as the Arabian peninsula, to visit Mecca, where he engaged in discussions

In the Sikh quarter of old Delhi, the faithful gather about a travelling exhibition devoted to Guru Nanak. Here Nanak is lecturing to his two faithful disciples, the Hindu Bala (left) and the Muslim Mardana (behind him).

with Muslim divines on the nature of Truth and the Supreme. In this holiest of all the Islamic cities, Nanak moved in the company of faquirs, and prayed at the Ka'ba, the focal point of Islamic worship. After that he traveled to Medina, where the Prophet Muhammad died, and then to Baghdad, the great seat of Arabic learning and studies. Here he paid his respects to a famous Muslim holy man, Hazrat Khwaja Behlol, both men sitting in complete silence in the wonder of the Divine, in perfect communion with each other. Nanak stayed for two weeks. After his departure, Hazrat Khwaja Behlol placed a plaque over the wall against which his visitor had sat to commemorate the event. The plaque read, "Here stayed Rab-i-Majid-Hazrat Baba Nanak," which meant, "Incarnation of the Almighty Himself."

In Persia, near the city of Tehran, Nanak encountered a group of Sufis. So close was he to them, and they to him, that the conversation was carried on by flashes of light. The Sufi master, after extended silence, finally asked, "What differentiates light from darkness?"

"There is no difference between light and darkness. Both are the same in eternity," said Nanak, for "Light envelops darkness, and darkness envelops light." He explained this cryptic remark with one of his verses:

> Losing the self is to become light.
> To assert the self is to become total darkness.
> It is self-assertion that transforms the light
>   into darkness.
> It is the light of love that envelops darkness
>   and transforms it back to light."

His travels continued almost relentlessly. He visited the remotest parts of the Himalayas, Afghanistan, the western Punjab, the Pathan strongholds and Sind, which were all Muslim, and the great centers of Hinduism — Hardwar, Mathura, Benares —

and on into Bihar and Bengal via the Ganges valley, and further into the dark tantric areas of Orissa and Assam. He may have visited south India and Ceylon. In all his travels into the centers of Brahminical Hinduism, the yogic retreats, the tantric caves, the monasteries of Sufis and the Muslim colleges and holy cities, he exhorted his listeners to discard barren ritual and false shows of piety, to concentrate on God-realization and to practice the deepest forms of humanitarianism. In all, he spent some twenty-five years on the road, and collected a tremendous number of disciples, or sishyas, from whom the word "Sikh" is derived. However, he did not preach renunciation of the world, as many holy men did, but called upon men to stay with their fellows, to fight the evils and injustices under which humanity was groaning, and to help bring about a just social order.

Though he met with much success, he also faced dangers and opposition. As he was returning from the Middle East to the Punjab, he and Bala and Mardana were captured by the Pathan ruler Ibrahim Lodhi and sentenced to death because they had preached a faith other than Islam. The three men spent seven months in a prison cell before being released, gaining their freedom when Ibrahim Lodhi was defeated and killed at the battle of Panipat by the Mogul leader Babar in 1526.

KABIR

Guru Nanak's teachings did not spring full-blown from his mind, but were the development of older doctrines and beliefs of a broad folk-based Hindu movement known as bhakti. Nanak was in the mainstream of the bhakti currents which flowed through India during the fifteenth century. Bhakti was an old, intense, deeply moving devotional Way popular among the common people of Hinduism for perhaps a thousand years or more. Briefly, it was the path of devotion to the Divine as opposed to the path of knowledge and ritual followed by the Brahmins, the Hindu priesthood. Bhakti centered upon love of a Supreme Person—expressed in the form of various Hindu deities, Vishnu or his incarnations Rama and Krishna, or Shiva, or the great mother Shakti—rather than a Supreme Abstraction, remote and unapproachable, silent and unreachable. In short, bhakti brought the ordinary people to direct access to the Lord by devotion to His person and in His mystical love. In bhakti one need not perform endless rites and rituals such as the priests practiced, nor need one endure the multitudinous rounds of births and rebirths—the karmic cycle—that the Brahmins believed was the fate of every man before liberation could be attained. Instead, through the love of the Divine, one could immediately become part of His warm, all-encompassing embrace in the joy of eternity. Bhakti also cut through the bounds of both caste and religion: many bhaktas, saints included, came from the lowest castes, and might be Muslims as well as Hindus. Bhakti inspired a tremendous amount of literature—devotional poems and hymns, theology, discourses, folk stories, popular sayings and philosophical treatises, plus much music and drama—centered on hundreds of incarnations of the gods, saints, heroes and heroines, and holy people of all walks of life, from the humblest potters and outcasts to kings and Brahmins.

Perhaps the greatest figure in the bhakti cults (for there were many) was the unique saint and poet Kabir, a low-caste weaver. Kabir was a germinal influence upon Nanak and the Sikhs, and was one of the great saints of India, popular with both Hindus and Muslims. His songs are still sung, and his poems and sayings form a good part of the folk wisdom of the Indian people.

Kabir was born in A.D. 1440, nineteen years before Nanak, in Benares, the great holy city on the Ganges in eastern India, and died in 1518. To make it clear that even Kabir is not free from legends, his most pious Hindu disciples say he was born in 1398 and passed away in 1527. Accounts differ about his birth, and there is, as may be expected, a fair number of details that strain Western credulity. Some sources state he was found as a babe lying on a lotus leaf in a village water tank near Benares. Though a Hindu, he was received into the Muslim community with appropriate rites and was named Kabir, the Great. Other sources believe he was a low-caste Hindu who became a weaver, by tradition in Benares a Muslim occupation, or was a Muslim who abandoned Islam at an early age to take up Hindu practices. For a while he followed the life of the typical wandering Hindu holy man, being received, though reluctantly, by a famous bhakta preacher named Ramananda, the disciple of a south Indian bhakta. Kabir "made bhakti popular in the seven continents and the nine regions" — that is, the whole world — according to an early biographer.

As a weaver by trade, Kabir was considered low-caste and of humble origin. He soon earned a reputation for mystical practices, performing miracles and preaching social equality. "None shall inquire into thy caste," he sang in a poem, "he who shall recite the name of the Lord will be claimed by Him." He drew upon forms of Hinduism centered upon worship of the god Vishnu and his incarnations but either rejected the polytheism of the faith or simplified it. He was also inspired by the mystical aspects of Islam. This fusion enabled Kabir to preach a universal religion of God indwelling in the heart of man, seeking a middle way between the excesses of Hinduism and the fierce dogmatism of Islam. He had a sharp wit and he ridiculed the ritualists. All ceremonies and formal worship, endless repetition of sacred texts and words, circumambulations around idols and the numerous prayers to the gods were, he said, a waste of time and energy.

> The beads are wood, the gods are stone.
> The Ganges and the Jumna [both sacred rivers] are water.
> Rama and Krishna are dead and gone,
> and the Vedas [the Hindu scriptures] are empty words.

[67]

Those who wished to worship God were to avoid the goat-faced, unkempt ascetics and the shaven-headed priests with empty religious discourses, to flee from the temples and the mosques, to seek Him in the fields, in the weaver's shop and in the happy home. Only fools would hope to find God in stones and buildings. "God is One, whether we worship Him as Allah or Rama," he said. "The Hindu God lives at Benares, the Muslim God at Mecca, but He who made the world lives not in a city made by hands. There is One Father of Hindu and Muslim, One God in all matter. He is the Lord of the earth."

> If thou are a true seeker,
> thou shall at once seek Me:
> Thou then shall meet me in a moment of time.
> Kabir says: O holy man!
> God is the breath of all breath.

Kabir, by practicing a trade and marrying (he was married twice and had several children), showed that one could live in the world and still be saintly. His example, his wit and his lively poems made him the most popular figure of his time. The result was that the ruling classes persecuted him. He was exiled from Benares, and with a band of followers wandered all over India, going as far as Afghanistan. His central teaching may be summarized in a passage from one of his own hymns:

The difference between faiths is only due to a difference in names; everywhere there is a yearning for the same god. Why do the Hindus and the Muslims quarrel for nothing? Keep at a distance all pride and vanity, insincerity and falsehood; consider others the same as yourself; let your heart be filled with love and devotion. Then alone will your struggle be fruitful. Life is but transitory, waste not your time, but take refuge in God. He is within your own heart, so why do you fruitlessly search him out in holy places, in scriptures, in rites and ceremonials?

[68]

Kabir's rejection of the formalities of both Hinduism and Islam was echoed in Nanak's teachings — that there was no Mecca for the Muslims and no Benares for the Hindus, but that God dwelt within, that it was not caste that sanctified one but one's own acts. So powerful a force was Kabir that many of his hymns were included in the Granth Saheb, the Sikh scripture.

There are no theological subtleties in Kabir, nor are there any in Nanak. Kabir taught the direct way to God, accessible to all men, for God dwelt within.

I close not my eyes, stop not my ears, nor torment my body.
But every path I then traverse becomes the path of pilgrimage.
Whatever work I engage in becomes service.
This simple consummation is the best.

In this body is the garden of Paradise;
within it are compressed the seven seas and the myriad stars;
here is the Creator manifest.

In every abode the light does shine;
it is you who are blind who cannot see.
When by the effort of continual looking you at length
     can see it,
the veils of this world will be torn apart.

Difficult is the Path leading to the Beloved:
it is like the edge of a sword.

The great wandering saint of India died in 1518, and upon his death both the Muslims and the Hindus claimed the body, the former to bury it according to their rites, and the latter to burn it. While the disciples were arguing for possession over the body, a celestial voice was heard commanding them to unwrap the shroud. Inside was nothing but a heap of flowers, which were equally divided between Muslims and Hindus, for burial and cremation, according to their respective customs.

At last, his travels completed, and age creeping upon him, Nanak settled down in the town of Sri Kartarpur (now on the Pakistani side of the line that divides the Punjab). Daily he would sit on the veranda before his house, or in the courtyard under a tree, while disciples flocked around, often just to look at him or to ask questions. (The mere seeing or being in the presence of a holy man is known as darshan and confers great spiritual benefit.) Some of his sayings from this period have been recorded. Most are simple and direct, in similes that the ordinary people could easily understand.

A disciple asked, "Why is it that I cannot dispel the illusion of Maya, that is, dark thoughts of self-pursuit?"

Nanak: "Look at your own shadow. Dear one, you can go for miles and miles and your shadow will always remain before you when you walk with the sun at your back. But the moment you turn your face to the sun, then where is the shadow?"

Another disciple asked what laws the Sikhs should follow if the Muslims follow their own laws, and the Hindus theirs.

Nanak: "The law of truth. There is no law higher than that nor any way of life superior to living truly, serving all those in need with love."

Finally, a yogi asked, "O Great Guru, why is it that in spite of my practicing the science of breath control in yoga my mind finds no peace?"

Nanak: "Dear friend, by hatha yoga you try to draw the energies of the Sun and the Moon into your physical system. Dear one, draw the energy from the sun within, and the mind will become as tranquil as the light from the moon."

This was Nanak's last public appearance. He was now sixty-nine (the year was 1538). His disciples knew instinctively this was to be his final day. After telling them to love each other — "There are a few who love those who love them, but a true devotee, a Sikh, must love all, even those who hate him" — he began to withdraw into himself, "within his Divine Self," says a Sikh writing. The disciples, seeing that their master was about to leave, began to weep bitterly and inconsolably. Nanak went into what is remembered as the Trance of Ascension. For a moment Nanak returned to the world to say:

> "Says Nanak, men weep truly indeed,
> O, Father of us all,
> when they weep through love."

Having chanted this verse, Nanak drew a white sheet over himself, and, according to tradition, ascended to the Supreme. Here a curious thing happened. As in the case of Kabir twenty years earlier, the Muslim devotees wanted the body in order to bury it and the Hindus wanted it to cremate it. But only the sheet remained, filled with flowers, which were enshrined under a dome at Kartarpur, the Muslims burying their share, the Hindus burning theirs. The Hindus later removed the ashes to the east bank of the Ravi River, which later became the boundary between India and Pakistan after Independence in 1947. Finally, after the Sikh warrior Ranjit Singh had unified the Sikhs by military conquest in the nineteenth century (they had been divided until then), the remains were installed at a shrine at Dera, about thirty-five miles from Amritsar, their sacred city.

THE GURUS

It was not likely that Nanak deliberately set about founding a new religious sect, but the events that followed his death shaped the Sikhs into a separate group. Shortly before he entered the Trance of Ascension, Nanak selected a devoted disciple named Lehna over one of his own sons to be the next leader of the community. Nanak changed Lehna's name to Angad, meaning "part of his own self." This led to the Sikh doctrine that all the Sikh gurus — there are only ten — are one in spirit, and are even called

Nanak, and that to look upon them as distinct would be heresy. In the basic Sikh scripture, the Granth Saheb, they are indicated separately by a mystic formula which would be rendered in English as The Bride of God, Guru Nanak being the First Bride, Angad the Second Bride and so on. In the words of another formula, "All ten gurus are revelations of one light and one form." They are also "one lamp lit from another" and so on. Angad assembled Nanak's own writings, which were considerable in volume. They were written in Punjabi in a newly devised script called Gurumukhi, which means "from the guru's mouth"; it is still the standard script for Punjabis. Angad also founded centers for disseminating Nanak's teachings.

The third guru, Amar Das (1479–1574) was seventy-nine when he was elected. He adapted Hindu festivals and ceremonies for the Sikhs, and further weakened the bonds of caste by establishing the common free kitchen, the langar. This was an important step, for caste Hindus will not eat food prepared by people of another caste. His son-in-law Ram Das (1534–1581) was chosen guru in 1574. He founded the city of Ramdaspur (named after himself); it was later called Amritsar and became the Sikhs' sacred city. Ram Das also laid the foundations for the Golden Temple, the center of Sikhism, which was surrounded by the sacred pool traditionally believed to have sprung from the earth in response to Nanak's command. Ram Das's son Arjun (1563–1606) was the fifth guru and one of the most important, for he edited the Granth Saheb (the final version was done by Govind Singh, the last guru).

The Granth Saheb, or Noble Book (it is also known as the Adi Granth, or First Book) was assembled from material not only from the first five Sikh gurus but from various Hindu and Muslim sources, among them Kabir. The work is written in six languages, including Punjabi and Hindi, the lingua franca of north India, and is arranged not by authors or languages but by thirty-one

A Sikh guru, or religious master. He wears the full beard of the traditional Indian holy man, the sannyasi; under his turban is his uncut hair, rolled into a topknot. As an ordinary guru, this man does not rank with the ten Gurus of the Sikhs, the divine leaders.

The Golden Temple at Amritsar, the center of Sikh worship. The temple was founded in the sacred pool in 1579 by Ram Das, the fourth Sikh Guru.

ragas, or musical modes, to which the hymns are set. It begins
with Nanak's Jap-ji, the key to Sikh spirituality and the epitome
of Sikh doctrines. The Jap-ji consists of a mul-mantra (or seed
prayer), which I have already quoted—it is the prayer Nanak
received during his enlightenment on the river bank—and
thirty-eight verses and a conclusion, called a shloka. The verses,
known as pauris, or rungs, contain the essence of Sikh belief and
present the five stages through which an individual must pass in
order to gain eternal bliss. These are: the Way of Duty and
Action; the Way of Knowledge; the Realm of Ecstasy; the Realm
of Power (where one loses the fear of death and is freed from the
round of births and rebirths); and lastly, the Abode of Truth,
where one is merged or absorbed into the Divine Being.

Guru Arjun's activities brought a reprisal from the tyrannical
Mogul emperor Jahangir, who had him tortured to death at La-
hore in 1606. Thus Arjun became the first of a line of Sikh
martyrs. By the attempts to repress them, the Sikhs were turned
from an assemblage of pastoral mystics into an army of warrior
mystics, becoming a militant, fearless, crusading anti-Muslim
brotherhood. Though he was only eleven when he became the
sixth guru, Arjun's son Har Govind organized his people into an
army. Armed clashes and even major battles with the Muslims
became a matter of course, the Sikhs being noted for their military skills and foolhardy, almost insane bravery in battle. (Even
today Sikhs are feared for their proneness to enter a mystical
berserk state at high noon in the fierce Punjabi sun and to run
amok while everyone takes to cover.) To symbolize the two aspects of the new type of Sikh guru, spiritual and secular, he was
to wear two swords.

The next three gurus, assuming leadership at early ages, were
Har Rai, Har Krishan and Teg Bahadur, all of whom were involved in the wars with the Moguls. Teg Bahadur was captured
by the forces of the Emperor Aurangzeb in 1675 and beheaded,

leaving his son, Govind Singh, only nine, to become the last guru. But Govind Singh was a genius and the greatest of the gurus after Nanak. He was highly educated in secular, martial and religious subjects. Govind revised or reformed Sikh rites. A major step was his announcement that after him there would be no more gurus, that the Granth Saheb was the Supreme Guru, the eternal Guru in whom all authority was inherent for all times future. Henceforth, also, a decision by the representatives of a majority of the community would be binding on everyone.

Govind's innovations were wide-ranging and unusual. He effected the final separation of the Sikhs from both Hindus and Muslims in a special rite on the Hindu New Year's day of 1699, when he initiated his five closest and favorite disciples, the Panj Pyaras (or the Five Beloved Ones), in a special rite that set them apart from the other religions of India. He was in turn initiated by them. All drank sweetened water stirred by a double-edged dagger from a communal bowl. Those assembled were a Brahmin, a kshatriya and three low-caste men, so this act destroyed the last vestiges of caste among the Sikhs, since it was not lawful for Hindus of different castes to drink from the same vessel for fear of incurring pollution. The rite also included the taking of new names. The suffix "Singh" (which means lion) was obligatory for all males; women are called Kaur (princess). The Sikhs adopted the five K's — unshorn hair and beard (kesh), a comb in the hair (kangh), a steel bangle on the right wrist (karah), short drawers (kacch), and a sword (kirpan). Hair was to be worn uncut, in the manner of the Indian holy men, such as sadhus and sannyasis, but the Sikhs cover it with a turban. Wearing long hair was one of the four rules of conduct, the others being prohibitions against alcohol and tobacco, certain types of meat and sexual relations with Muslim women.

Sikhs who follow the five K's and the four rules are known as khalsa, or pure. Their ideal is that of the warrior-saint, fearless in battle for the protection of the community and devoted to God—mystics ready to fight like lions. "When all other means have failed, it is righteous to draw the sword," said Govind Singh, for he had "trained the sparrow to hunt the hawk" and "one man to fight a legion."

Govind Singh was murdered by a Pathan soldier in the Mogul's armies, but his spirit remained to inspire his people. War became the joy and the pastime of the community, and the most fearless were known as the Akalis, the Deathless. The quiet devotional faith of Guru Nanak was turned into one of the most powerful forces of aggression. The military history of the Sikhs is outside the scope of this chapter, but it should be mentioned that early in the nineteenth century their greatest general, Ranjit Singh— "short, deformed, blind in one eye, illiterate," but a great leader of men—organized all the diverse groups among the Sikhs and became master of the Punjab and of Afghanistan and Kashmir as well. Immediately upon his death his successors declared war on the British, those great despoilers of the continent. But the foreigners won in two dreadful battles and ten years after Ranjit Singh's death (in 1839), the British had broken Sikh power and taken over the Punjab.

THE TEACHINGS

We have seen that Sikhism is a way that is devotional and not philosophical or theological. Ideally, Sikhism teaches and preaches a strong monotheism. That is virtually the first statement a Sikh will make. "There is one God, Eternal Truth is His name," said Nanak, in a phrase echoed by his successors and repeated in various forms in the Granth Saheb and other scriptures. In the oneness of God is the fellowship of man. All the gurus declare that the aim and end of life is not primarily to seek a heavenly abode (though that will come), but to develop the Essence within and thus merge with God. The Sikhs reject the

Hindu concept of God incarnating Himself—the idea of the avatar—on earth, yet the gurus are almost such incarnations. But God is distinct from mankind. "He lives in everything, He dwells in every heart. Yet He is not merged with anything. He is separate, He lives in all, yet is ever distinct. He abides with thee, too. As fragrance dwells in a flower or a reflection in a mirror, so does God dwell inside everything. Seek Him therefore in the Heart."

Yet one finds countless references to the Hindu deities, among them Brahma, Durga, Shiva and similar gods. Sikh monotheism becomes affected by the surrounding Hindu polytheism, and by Hindu customs and practices. Caste, so emphatically rejected by the Sikhs, surfaces as they mix with, work with and marry Hindus. When a Sikh man marries a Hindu woman, it is her devotional practices that enter the Sikh home. And the Hindu concept of birth and rebirth, often rejected or softened among the Sikhs, still returns to affect their beliefs. The Hindu faith in rebirth until past misdeeds and evil acts are purified through countless transmigrations is basic to Sikhism, but to it is joined the Muslim concept of God's absolute domination and the equally important concept of free will. "According to the seed we sow is the fruit we reap," says the Granth Saheb. "By the will of God, O Nanak, man must either be saved or endure new births."

Nirvana—final liberation—comes when "through the grace of the Guru a man dies to self and is born to new understanding, then the soul is free from its soiling and is not born again."

Despite their small numbers—a mere two percent of India's six hundred million—the Sikhs are a very visible presence in today's India. In the past century, once they had come to terms with European domination, their martial abilities made them an important part of the British armies in both World Wars. Today they are said to furnish half the officer ranks of the Indian army and a

The Sikh symbol, the Ek Oankar, which contains the names of the Supreme Being. Ek Oankar is written in the Gurumukhi alphabet, with the numeral I followed by the nasalized vowel for 0 (or Om), signifying the unity and indivisibility of God.

large percentage of the ordinary ranks. They are also great athletes, and some of India's Olympic teams have been half Sikh.

The Sikhs are still concentrated in their original homeland, the Punjab, which contains eighty percent of all the Sikhs of India. The rest are spread about, primarily in the Punjab's neighboring states, but one can find Sikhs anywhere, intelligent, aggressive, humorous, and still observing Nanak's plan for an entire community in the tradition of the Indian holy man, the sannyasi. In today's world the Sikhs have adapted to modern ways and modern machines. They are skilled operators of engines—many of the Indian pilots are Sikhs, and Sikhs less endowed may become truck or taxi drivers, driving with the same fiery, fierce élan with which they swept on horseback across the Punjab plains, first against the Muslims and then against the Afghans and the English. But these are nonessentials. It is Nanak's vision that dominates. Many Sikhs still arise at three in the morning, bathe and then meditate upon the name of God, and recite the compositions of the Gurus as daily prayers. Service to fellow beings is an essential duty of the Sikhs as a practical expression of love. One of the ways in which Sikhs serve is by working at the temples, called gurudwaras, or "Guru's door." Service takes the form of sweeping the temple's floors, cleaning utensils, getting water from the wells and working in the free kitchen, the langar, where everyone is fed in token of the abolition of the distinctions of caste and rank.

Fearless, independent, mystical, the Sikh is an individual apart, proud yet humble before the Lord, willing to die if necessary for the faith. Only the Sikh who can risk his life can be saved. "In this street," said Nanak, referring to the Path of loving service to the Lord, "walk with your head placed upon your palm." The Sikh is not to fear martyrdom for the cause of God. "Dying is not an evil," adds Nanak, "the death of heroic men is blessed. The true hero is he who in defense of the helpless may be hacked from limb to limb but does not flee the field."

4

CHINA:
TAOISM AND
CONFUCIANISM

A long time ago there was a person known as the Yellow Ancestor. Though he appears in the writings of several schools of Chinese thought, he is a special favorite of the Taoists, followers of that mystical, anarchistic Way who thought even in the distant past that mankind was getting too much of a bad thing, civilization and government. The Taoists saw the Yellow Ancestor as a symbol not only of the good aspects of mankind but also of its stupidity. The Yellow Ancestor, who is the legendary source of the human race, is known primarily from a lost work, the *Book of the Yellow Ancestor*, which survives in quotations and anecdotes in Taoist books, especially in the famous *Chuang tzu* of the fourth century B.C.

The Yellow Ancestor (sometimes called the Yellow Emperor or the Yellow Ruler) is the title of Huang Ti, the third of the legendary emperors of times past. The Chinese have quite accurate historical records from fairly early times (though not so early as the Egyptians and the Sumerians), beginning with the Sage Kings

Yao (?2357–2258 B.C.) and Shun (?2255–2208 B.C.). Every ruler of the various states is accounted for, except for Fu Hsi, the Conqueror of Animals; Shen Nung, the Divine Husbandman; and Huang Ti, the Yellow Ancestor, all of whom are mentioned in early works. Because they could not be slipped into the records of known rulers, the trio were assigned to the (questionable) period 2698–2599 B.C., an age in which people throughout China were just beginning to adopt civilized ways.

Fu Hsi, besides domesticating animals (a major step toward a civilized life), is also credited with having invented the eight trigrams that make up the sixty-four hexagrams used in the I Ching, the Book of Changes, which has so endeared itself to Western hearts and minds in recent years. Fu Hsi was followed by Shen Nung, who, as the Divine Husbandman, taught the Chinese how to till the soil with the plow. His descendants were conquered by the Yellow Ancestor, the grandfather of the Chinese race.

It was the Yellow Ancestor who taught some of the basic doctrines of Tao, that ineluctable, mysterious, ineffable Way that escapes definition. We don't know if the Yellow Ancestor had worked out the teachings, or if they arose spontaneously and instinctively out of his soul, but he is credited with some of the earliest beliefs. One of the doctrines of Tao is that to climb is to fall: one must be unobtrusive. Like water, Tao seeks the low ground, the valley. But in the valley there is life, the water spirit, or the Mysterious Female, said the Yellow Ancestor.

> The Valley Spirit never dies.
> It is named the Mysterious Female
> And the Doorway of the Mysterious Female
> is the base from which Heaven and Earth sprang.
> It is there within us all the while;
> draw upon it as you will, it never runs dry.

*One must be still like the waters in the valley: to a mind that is still, the entire cosmos surrenders. The soul is restored not by effort but by doing nothing. An anecdote about the Ancestor explains how.

On an excursion to the Red Lake and the K'un-lun Mountains, the emperor lost his black pearl while gazing south to the place from which he had come and to which he would return. He asked Wisdom to find it, without success. And then in turn, he asked Keen Vision and Skilled Debater, neither of whom could find the pearl. Then the Yellow Ancestor requested Nothing (literally, Nothing-seeming) to search, and Nothing found it. "Strange indeed," said the Ancestor, "that Nothing was able to find it."

The point, of course, is that he who strives does not succeed, while he who does Nothing attains all. According to the Taoists, the first to tamper with men's hearts and minds was the Yellow Ancestor when he taught goodness and duty, which were the virtues preached centuries later by Confucius and his followers. In obedience to these teachings the Sage Kings Yao and Shun slaved for their people until there was no hair on their shanks and no fuzz on their thighs, and they wore out their guts in endless acts of goodness and duty and depleted their energies in establishing laws and regulations for the populace. But none of these made the people good; tyrants, robbers, thieves and brigands abounded, charlatans and honest men fought with each other, and in short, bad went to worse. The *Chuang tzu* says:

> The philosophers confused themselves about joy and anger, deceived themselves about stupidity and wisdom, criticized themselves about good and evil, and maligned themselves about falsehood and truth, the world began to decline. Excellence in all its grandeur lost its equality, and life itself slipped away. The world grew fond of know-how, and the people sought to exhaust it. Axes and saws served as laws, plumb lines determined death, awls and chisels formed judgments. The world went straight to pieces.

The blame, said the Taoist sage Lao Tzu, "lies in the initial

[83]

binding of men's hearts and minds by Yellow Ancestor." The
Yellow Ancestor realized how his attempts at putting the world in
shape had failed. He went to see a mountain sage, who told him
he talked too much. The Ancestor went into the wilderness,
living there for three months. A second visit to the sage brought
him the admonition to let the inner spirit take over, not to agitate
himself, not to be concerned with what went on around him.
"Preserve your body carefully," said the sage, who himself had
lived twelve hundred years. The sage told the Ancestor about
Tao:

> The quintessence of Tao is dark and obscure. The pinnacle of
> Tao is dimness and silence . . . Tao is infinite, but everyone thinks
> of Tao as finite. Tao is unfathomable, though everyone thinks in
> terms of high and low points.

Taoism, according to tradition, was actually founded by Lao Tzu,
also known as Lao Tan, or Old Big Ear. He lived from 604 to 531
B.C. if he lived at all, for there is some doubt that he was an
actual person. At any rate, the *Lao tzu*, the work which bears his
name (it is also called the *Tao te ching*), and in which he is the
central character, contains the story of Taoism, though the seeds
of it go back to legendary times, even to the Yellow Ancestor himself. The *Lao tzu* is the summary of the author's knowledge,
though Old Big Ear clearly did not write the entire work himself,
and it obviously contains not only his own beliefs but those of the
hoary past.

The legend behind the *Lao tzu* is interesting. By all signs Lao
Tzu was a crusty old individual who tolerated no interference in
his very private way of life. In his old age, conditions in his part of
China reached such a bad state that he ran away from home,
riding on a black ox. As he crossed the mountains into the safety
of a neighboring kingdom, he was stopped by an individual known
as the Keeper of the Pass, who asked him to write down the total

of his knowledge. This Lao Tzu did in some five thousand concise Chinese characters. Traditionally, the work was written in two parts, one called the *Tao ching*, the other the *Te ching*, so the book is sometimes called the *Tao te ching*, though it is best known as the *Lao tzu*. Eventually Lao Tzu, his anger at his own people abated, returned home to pass his final years in study and meditation. As noted before, whether or not he actually wrote the work that bears his name is a question for scholars. The final form does not seem to have been given to the book until the second century B.C., and to experts it is clearly a compilation from several sources.

The second most important Taoist work (there are many) is the *Chuang tzu* (or *Chuang chou*), which is named after an individual, who again, like Lao Tzu, might possibly be legendary. Again, the *Chuang tzu* is a compilation, and it carries on the tradition of Lao Tzu, both man and book, in laying out what Tao is and is not.

What Tao is not is more easily defined than what it is, for Tao is taken by the Taoists as essentially metaphysical, eternal, all-pervading, inexhaustible, fathomless, the source of all things. There are no precise translations for the Chinese ideograms that are connected with Tao, though their equivalents may range from an abstract First Principle to Primal Source to a mystical Cosmic Mother, or Mysterious Female. The word "Tao" is sometimes translated by Westerners as God, but God in the Judeo-Christian-Islamic sense Tao is not. The word is also used by the Confucians. To try to avoid some of the confusion, the Confucian tao will not be capitalized, for it is ethical in sense and deals with a way of life and with daily philosophical and moral problems. But one is always on slippery ground in dealing with Tao and tao, and occasionally we may find the Confucians, who survived a long time, using the term in the same sense as the Taoists, their enemies.

The central fact of Tao is that it cannot be defined, for the *Lao tzu* states that "The way that can be spoken of is not the constant way," and, "The way is forever nameless." Moreover, "The way conceals itself in being nameless." Yet one always tries to grapple with, to pin down the ineffable. Chuang Tzu warns that "Tao cannot be conveyed by either words or silence. In that state which is neither speech nor silence its transcendental nature may be apprehended," a mood that parallels that of Hindu metaphysics.

In the end, one adopts a Taoist point of view: What does Tao say of itself? Thus, some phrases from various sources of Tao speaking about Tao:

Great Tao is like a boat that drifts: it can go this way, it can go that.

Tao is real, is faithful, yet does nothing and has no form. Can be handed down, yet cannot be passed from hand to hand, can be got but cannot be seen. It is its own trunk, its own root.

One need not peep through the window to see Tao, Tao is not there. The further one goes away from himself, the less he knows.

Tao is all-pervading, and its use is inexhaustible.
Fathomless, like the fountain head of all things,
Its sharp edges rounded off, its tangles untied.
Its light tempered, its turmoil submerged.

Yet crystal clear like still water it seems to remain.
I do not know whose Son it is,
An image of what existed before the Heavenly Ruler.

The sensible middle way of the Taoists' rivals, the Confucians, with their emphasis on goodness and righteousness or morality (remember the Yellow Ancestor's error), was an affront to the Taoists. They saw man and the universe, all life, as a unit, while the Confucians fitted everything into a hierarchy with each part connected and interrelated, responsible to those above and below.

[86]

For the Confucian, human society and civilization were an earthly mirror of the cosmic tao. But a hierarchical society, no matter how perfect, was, to the Taoists, a crime against the natural order of the universe. Before the Confucians came to straighten things out, as Chuang Tzu said, man was in a state of pure simplicity, without knowledge, free from desires and of a natural virtue. "The nature of people was what it ought to be"— simple and easygoing. Then the sagely men, the Confucians, appeared, "limping and wheeling about in human-heartedness, pressing along and standing on tip-toe in the doing of righteousness." The Confucians went to excess in hacking up materials (the waste of both clay and jade are mentioned) to make sacrificial vessels and their objects of culture, leisure and commerce. The answer to the chaos caused by "order" was, as the *Lao tzu* said:

> Banish wisdom, discard knowledge,
> And the people will be benefited a hundredfold.
> Banish human-heartedness, discard morality,
> and the people will be dutiful and compassionate.
> Banish skill, discard profit,
> and thieves and robbers will disappear.
>
> Give them Simplicity to look at,
> the Uncarved Block to hold.
> Give them selflessness and fewness of desires.

The Taoists were convinced that the Confucians lost Tao, substituting power in its place, after which their other two qualities of human-heartedness and morality were lost, being replaced by ritual. But "ritual is the mere husk of loyalty and promise-keeping and is indeed the first step toward brawling." The Confucian middle way—the Way of the Mean—which states that the prosperity of each brings the prosperity of all, and that the general prosperity brings the prosperity of the individual, in effect

A second-century B.C. *tomb rubbing shows a famous but possibly apocryphal meeting between Confucius and Lao Tzu. Confucius is at the left, with a pheasant for the testy Lao Tzu. Confucius began to expound*

on the books he had written but the Taoist sage cut him off and told him
he talked too much. "What you are doing," he told Confucius, "is to
disjoint men's nature."

implies a "team enterprise." But the Taoists saw it as a kind of totalitarian society, with the philosopher sages instructing everyone, from the ruler on down, from a vantaged position, on the fulfillment of duties, rites and obligations. Confucianism is the modern age to perfection—building roads, founding towns, establishing markets, making laws and regulations, all for the betterment of the people. But Taoism is a kind of counterculture, an alternate culture. The material world has no great importance for the Taoist, for Tao is "the very progenitor of all things in the world. In it sharpness is blunted, all tangles untied, all glare tempered, all dust smoothed. It is like a pool that never dries." The Taoist goes by himself, without schools, hierarchy, adepts, disciples. The Taoist's heart must be free from all desire and he must travel through desolate wilds.

> I will leave you and enter the gate of the Unending, to enjoy myself in the fields of the illimitable. I will blend my light with that of the sun and moon, and will endure while heaven and earth endure. If men agree with my views, I will be unconscious of it; if they keep apart from them, I will be unconscious of it; they may all die, and I will abide alone.

> Far to the south there is a place called the Land where Tê Rules. [Tê is roughly the idea of potentiality in this usage.] Its people are ignorant and unspoiled, negligent of their own interests and of few interests, and of few desires. They know how to make, but not how to hoard. They give but seek no return. The subtleties of decorum, the solemnities of ritual are alike unknown to them. They live and move thoughtlessly and at random, yet every step they take tallies with the Great Plan. They are ready to enjoy life while it lasts, are ready to be put away when death comes. I would have you leave your kingdom and its ways, take Tao as your guide and travel to this land.

In the Taoists' works there are vague references to a secret discipline which closely resembles Indian yoga. There are ways of sitting and breathing, of looking with the eyes half closed and unfocused, and unspecified mentions of inner states which seem to be identical with that of samadhi, the highest stage of yoga, in which the mind, or the self, is absorbed in the Absolute. Taoist literature is vague, and undoubtedly Chinese yoga was an esoteric practice, taught secretly within a special circle which passed down the lore from master to pupil, confining it to the most likely candidates. Lao Tzu was reported sitting "so utterly motionless that one could not believe a human being was there at all . . . stark and lifeless as a withered tree." The *Chuang tzu* gives the case of a man named Ch'i who went into an ecstatic state or trance resembling samadhi: Ch'i was sitting against a low table when "He looked up to heaven and his breath died down. Without a sound he seemed to lose his partnership of soul and body." A disciple thought Ch'i's body "like a sapless tree" and "his mind like dead ashes." Ch'i eventually awakened and said, "When you saw me just now, my self was gone clean away." A few other cases are mentioned in Taoist literature, not as something unusual, but as if "yoga" was common but not to be discussed often in public. The Taoists seemed to go off on an inner voyage. A common term for this was "yu," to wander or travel. The Confucians used yu in the sense of wandering from court to court, but for the Taoists it was an esoteric journey. "He whose sightseeing is inward can find in himself all he needs. Such is the highest form of traveling, while it is a poor sort of journey that depends on outside things." A Taoist named Hu-chi'iu Tzu said, "The greatest traveler does not know where he is going, the greatest sightseer does not know what he is looking at. His travels do not take him to one part of creation more than another; his sightseeing is not directed to one sight rather than another."

THE GOLDEN FLOWER

Among the many curious Taoist works is one known as *The Secret of the Golden Flower*. One may be alternately charmed and baffled by it, for it is one of the few documents that openly mention

techniques of Chinese "yoga." Yet even with the book, one needs
a master, for most of it is in a kind of code which only the initiate
can understand. Yet, more than Lao Tzu's *Tao te ching* or the
Chuang tzu or any of the many lesser writings, it offers a key to
the locked box of esoteric practices enjoyed by the Taoists.

The Secret of the Golden Flower was discovered by the German
Sinologist Richard Wilhelm who came across it in a shop in
Peking in 1920. The work had been transmitted orally for centuries, until the 1600s, when it was printed in an edition of type
carved in wooden blocks. A second edition came out about two
centuries later, and then a nineteenth-century version in which
the title was changed to *The Art of Prolonging Human Life* by its
latest publisher.

The oral tradition dates back to the eighth century A.D. to the
religion of the Golden Elixir of Life, founded, according to tradition, by a Taoist adept, Lü Yen, sometimes known as Lü the
Guest of the Cavern. The sect, like other Taoist movements since
the second century B.C., was esoteric and secret, and became
more so as its members were accused of political intrigue. In 1891
the Manchus murdered some fifteen thousand members. Lü himself credited the origin of his knowledge to the legendary Kuan
Yin-hsi, the Keeper of the Pass, the same man who had requested
Lao Tzu to write out a summary of his knowledge. By the time of
Lü Yen, Taoism had acquired an unfortunate number of magical
and alchemical accretions, and his sect was a movement of
purification.

The Secret of the Golden Flower, bafflingly simple at first, is in
fact highly complex and sophisticated. It is a manual of meditation, and involves quite literal instructions in sitting, breathing,
posture, the fixing of the heart and other aids to concentration.
The goal is to develop "Circulation of the Light" in order to attain
readiness for "the Far Journey." We are on familiar ground in
many places in the text, for Lü states, "That which exists
through itself is called Tao."

A block from The Secret of the Golden Flower shows the initial steps in meditation, by which the devotee is to develop "Circulation of the Light" in preparation for the "Far Journey."

Tao has neither name nor force. It is the one essence, the one primordial spirit. Essence and life cannot be seen. It is contained in the Light of Heaven. The Light of Heaven cannot be seen. It is contained in the two eyes.

Lü explains that the Golden Flower is the Light, but merely as an image, for "It is the true power of the transcendent Great *One*," explaining that the Great *One* is the term given to that which has nothing above it. The Far Journey leads to the land that is nowhere, for "that is the true home." There is some Buddhist influence in the work, and a few scholars have seen even Zoroastrian and Christian doctrines of the most esoteric sort within its pages. When the disciple receives the ultimate truth, Lü warns, "Keep it secret and hold to it strictly."

Originally Taoism, though mystical and esoteric, was not superstitious. But throughout ancient China there was much on the folk level, and even in the courts, that was simply shamanistic, superstitious and magical. Spirits and demons had to be appeased and propitiated, the dead honored, the future feared. Great natural forces — famines, earthquakes, floods — threatened mankind. There was a great reliance upon sorcerers and occult practitioners, especially the class of women known as wu, who were shamanesses and feared and respected for their powers. By the second century B.C., four centuries after Lao Tzu, the tenets of "pure" Taoism were followed by a few, but Taoism itself had been taken over by the superstitious and the wonder workers, for its mysticism implied great occult powers for the initiate. Taoism in general — if one could actually use the term "Tao" in this sense — became a group of churches that had drawn folk beliefs and practices into Lao Tzu's Tao. Magic mirrors, charms, amulets, spells, bells, secret writings, occult rites and other such practices turned Taoism into uncritical forms of superstition.

[94]

In later centuries a number of movements — some merely expressing new byways in Tao, others attempting to purify it — began to multiply. An early development was the Way of the Five Bushels of Rice (so called after the price of admission to the sect), otherwise known as the Principal One sect, founded by Chan Tao Ling in the second century A.D. Chan styled himself the Master of Heaven, and passed on both his title and his spirit to his successors. The sect was established on Dragon Tiger mountain in Kiangsi province. Its members, who included both celibate monks and married laymen, were noted as master sorcerers, and were often called to the courts to advise on matters of handling natural disasters or future policies of war and peace. The most recent Master of Heaven, the sixty-fourth of the line, was installed in 1970 in Taiwan. Sects continued to multiply; among those beginning in the thirteenth and fourteenth centuries A.D. were the Perfecting the True sect, a vegetarian movement close to Lao Tzu's ideals, and the Pervading-Unity sect, which taught that the world is in the midst of a catastrophic age but will be saved by Old Mother Transcending Life. Virtually all the sects were secret and esoteric, guarding principles and beliefs carefully but often trying to influence the courts. As recently as World War II a new sect, the Hall of Tao, brought in elements from Confucianism, Buddhism, Christianity and Islam, and preached world brotherhood.

The Taoist sects were dealt a serious blow with the democratic revolution of 1911, which ousted the Manchus and tried to bring China into the modern world. In 1949 Mao Tse-tung formally proscribed all secret organizations, including the Taoist sects, and arrested those who did not abandon their beliefs. But curiously, in 1957, under the formal auspices of the Communist government, the Chinese Taoist Association was organized at Peking; its first meeting brought together former monks and nuns from all over the country. The aim of the Association was to unite

Taoists again, to promote the ancient doctrines and to support the socialist reconstruction of the country. But since then, the Way of the Tao in the twentieth century A.D. is as it was in the sixth century B.C., when Lao Tzu said: "I am as serene as the ocean, as mobile as the wind." For "to remain detached from all outside things is the climax of oneness. To have in oneself no contraries is the climax of purity." If the Way of the Tao exists, or does not exist, only Tao itself knows. The Tao man is the Supreme Man, the True Man, the Man of Supreme Inward Power: "His soul is intact."

> The great bushlands are ablaze, but he feels no heat, the River and the Han stream are frozen over but he feels no cold. Fierce winds break the hills, winds rock the ocean but he is not startled. He can climb high and not stagger, go through water and not get wet, go through fire and not be scorched.

CONFUCIANISM

Confucius is possibly the best known of all the world's sages, and many sayings and gems of wisdom, some of them comic and obviously spurious, are attributed to him. "Confucius" is a latinization of K'ung-fu-tzu, his Chinese title, which means Master Kung. His proper name, which is rarely used, was K'ung Ch'iu. K'ung was the family name, and Ch'iu meant hill, a name given to him because at birth he had a bulge on his skull. His given name became a sacred word and was seldom mentioned by the Chinese.

Confucius was born in 551 B.C. of an aristocratic family that had suffered much privation and hardship. His father, a minor military official, at seventy married his wife, a young girl of only seventeen, and died three years after his son's birth. The child, Ch'iu, was raised by his mother alone. She is known from the old documents to have been a strong-willed, courageous woman, who indoctrinated her son with respect for the court and for the wisdom of the past. The Chinese have a great respect for the facts, and as well have a clear sense of history, so what we know about the Sage, unlike the strange hagiography that accompanies other ancient figures, bears the clear mark of reality. One of his biographers, Sse-ma Ch'ien, who lived during the first century B.C., assembled the known material about the Sage, confining it largely to hard facts. In place of giving us unbelievable stories about Confucius's birth and infancy to account for his sagacity and saintliness, Sse-ma wrote simply that "Confucius was always wont to set up sacrificial vessels in his childish way, and to imitate ceremonial gestures."

There is some confusion in Sse-ma about the date when Confucius joined government service, but this is a minor point. Probably he was about twenty at the time; he had recently married (he was the father of one son and at least one daughter), and his mother had just died. But the young Sage served with honor. "Confucius was poor and of low estate and when he grew older he served as petty official of the family Chi and while he was in office his accounts and the measures were always correct. Thereupon he was made Chief Shepherd; then the beasts grew and multiplied." In his retelling of the Sage's life Sse-ma added the odd information that "Confucius was nine feet six inches tall. All the people called him a giant and marvelled at him." Confucius served under a number of rulers, sometimes with success, sometimes falling into disfavor because of court intrigues. One of the regular complaints against him was his insistence on the proper performance of ceremonies at court and the observing of the rules of decorum. The simple fact was that the various kings often liked having Confucius around as a sign of their interest in leading a proper life but resented his attempts to put his teachings into practice.

Despite his troubles with the rulers, Confucius attracted a

large group of disciples and followers. The exact number is not clear, but throughout his life he may have had as many as three thousand. He instructed them on a personal basis in four subjects: literature, conduct, conscientiousness and loyalty. At one point, because of the chaotic conditions of the times and his troubles with the kings, Confucius decided to go into retirement, for "from the highest dignitaries down, everyone was grasping of power and all had deserted the true way."

One of his most intense personal interests was music. He played the Chinese zither, and his musical studies were a source of strength during his exile. He was politely neutral about most subjects, but music produced strong opinions. He first rejected the music of the state of Shao because he thought it was "wanton," but later heard it under more favorable conditions, and his biographer remarks, "for three months he did not notice the taste of his food." "I never imagined music had reached such a height," said Confucius.

The Sage eventually returned to government service, but his reputation for honesty and probity, and his beneficial effects upon others — he was a great hero of the common people — brought the constant suspicion in the courts that he was only seeking his own aggrandizement. The rulers of the corrupt and chaotic states could not understand the altruistic motives of a man who put the well-being of others ahead of his own interests.

Confucius may have been too self-effacing. He did not believe in being an innovator, preferring to base his teachings on the past, which he thought had been a kind of a golden age. Only by returning to the best of the past could the present and future be possible. The wisdom of the ancients contained all that was necessary for a man. "I communicate and do not invent," he said. "I have faith in antiquity and consecrate all my affection to its cause." He had a clear vision of society, a society in which every person had his place in a great pyramid which pointed to the Son of Heaven, the emperor. It was incumbent upon each person in the hierarchy to fit in according to the best of his or her ability.

The Sage's probity may have been annoying to many people. The picture we got of him is of a narrow, formal, humorless, didactic individual, who pressed ceremony and formality to the breaking point. One of his disciples said:

> Among his own country people, Confucius wore a homely look, like one who has no word to say. In the ancestral temple and at court, his speech was full but cautious. At court he talked frankly to men of low rank, winningly to men of high rank. In the king's presence he looked intent and solemn. When bearing the sceptre, his back bent, as under too heavy a burden. He held his hands not higher than in bowing, nor lower than in giving a present. He wore an awed look, and dragged his feet as though they were bound.

> He did not eat much. He did not talk at meals, nor speak when in bed. His stables having been burned, the Master on his return from court said, "Is anyone hurt?" He did not ask after the horses. When summoned by the king, he walked without waiting for his carriage. When a friend died who had no home to go to, he said, "It is for me to bury him." When a friend sent a gift, even of a carriage and horses, he did not bow. He bowed only for sacrificial meat.

HIS TEACHINGS

The Chinese word for the teachings of Confucius and the system or school founded upon them is Ju. Initially, during the period in which Confucius lived, the word meant a scholar or intellectual, and the term then had the connotation of "weakling." The ju's function at court was to direct or assist the performances of the various ceremonies and rites, both secular and religious. In later centuries Ju came to contain much material other than that propounded by Confucius. Confucianism is not a religion in the Judeo-Christian-Islamic or Hindu-Buddhist sense but is both a philosophy pure and simple and an ethical code directed to right living. The emphasis is on a rational, tightly structured, hierarchical society of unparalleled honesty, with due allowance for the vagaries of human nature, which Confucius observed with the skill of a psychologist. "Look at a man's acts," he said. "Watch his motives: find out what pleases him. Can the man evade you?" In another context he noted, "Maids and servants are hardest to keep in your house. If you are friendly with them, they lose their deference; if you are reserved with them, they resent it."

Filial piety is the core of Confucianism. And this piety is served by obedience. One must be materially obedient, helping and serving one's parents and honoring them, and then when they die, laying them to rest with propriety and the proper sacrifices. Filial piety is the pivot on which the societal pyramid balances or hangs. This piety is applied outside the home to one's clan or extended family, to the officials of the state and to the ruler himself, who is bound to the heavens. And the chain descends downward, for one's underlings must be treated with the proper respect and sense of proportion.

The six works which are generally credited to Confucius (he was editor or compiler and commentator rather than author) contain matter that outlines his own beliefs. They are collections of ethical sayings and prescriptions, rules for ceremonies, songs, historical data (of the barest sort) and his commentaries on the *I Ching*, the Book of Changes. His works contain his lofty conceptions of simple virtues: faithfulness to one's self and to others (chung), altruism (shu), human-heartedness (jen), righteousness (yi), propriety (li), wisdom (chih), sincerity (hsin), all qualities which Confucius himself tried to exemplify. This insistence on moral and ethical cultivation was for Confucius a way of life, of truth, which he called tao. This tao is not the Tao of the Taoists, but a moral law applicable to man based on the correctness of human relationships, a law serving mankind just as a natural law served Heaven. And this law was one of a middle way — later to be called the Doctrine of the Mean — which was easily evident in the sayings attributed to the Sage.

The noble man first practices what he preaches and then preaches what he practices.

A superior man considers what is right; a vulgar man considers what will pay.

Loveless men cannot bear need long, they cannot bear fortune long. Loving hearts find peace in love.

A man without virtue cannot long abide in adversity, nor can he long abide in happiness.

If the ruler himself is upright, all will go well even though he does not give orders. But if he himself is not upright, even though he gives orders, they will not be obeyed.

HIS LAST YEARS

As he turned sixty, Confucius realized that he could not live many years longer. He began to assemble the wisdom that he considered reflected his own beliefs, and shortly he withdrew from public life to concentrate on his studies. The works generally attributed to him are the following:

The Book of History (sometimes called the Book of Records). It is concerned with the regulations of wise rulers and the meditations of their faithful ministers, and includes some vague references to a primitive astronomic religion ruled by a priest king. Scholars are in doubt about the accuracy and authenticity of the present text, for all the ancient manuscripts were burned in the third century B.C., and the text was constructed from oral tradition.

The Book of Odes, a collection of 305 songs winnowed from a vast library of some three thousand. Only the texts (and in some cases merely the titles) have been kept. The work runs from simple folk pieces to ceremonial and religious music.

Record of Rites. A fragmented selection of court rituals and songs based upon more archaic texts, with much post-Confucian material that is in the Sage's own tradition.

The Book of Changes (the famous *I Ching*). This is one of the most important works. It is a well-preserved and very ancient work from both Taoist and folklorist sources, with numerous later additions. The Sage's contributions are not clear, but parts of the commentaries may either be his own or those of his immediate followers, who have worked in his observations during lectures. Confucius himself considered the *I Ching* to be one of the most important of all texts, expressing the opinion that because of its sacred and mystical nature it should be approached only by those of mature years. He stated that he wished he had fifty years in which to study it.

Spring and Autumn Annals. A bare-bones account of events in the state of Lu, his own land, in which, by the prominence he gives an event, Confucius makes his own judgment on the individuals concerned.

The final Confucian work is the Analects, a collection of his sayings originally assembled by his disciples and added to and edited by later generations. In it we can see his hierarchical view of society, with the ruler setting the moral and ethical code for the kingdom.

Despite the straightforward accounts of the Sage's life by Sse-ma and others, a few incredible events creep in. A fabulous animal, the ch'i lin (which roughly resembles a dog in shape) is said to have appeared to his mother before his birth. Sometime after his seventieth birthday, while hunting with a companion, Confucius saw a ch'i lin; he remarked, 'My career is at an end," and he went into full retirement. About this time he openly expressed some mystical thoughts similar to the ideas espoused by the Taoists. If he had such yearnings earlier they were not recorded.

"No one knows me!" he lamented to a disciple, Tze Kung. His disciple asked what he meant. Confucius said, "I do not murmur against Heaven, I do not grumble against man. I pursue my studies here on earth, and am in touch with Heaven above. It is Heaven that knows me."

In 480 B.C., at seventy-two, Confucius became gravely ill. When Tze Kung visited him later, Confucius said, in terms that echo the hexagrams of the I Ching:

> The Sacred Mountain caves in,
> the roof beam breaks,
> the Sage will vanish.

Then he added, in the same mystical vein:

> For a long time the world has been unregulated. No one understood how to follow me. The people of Hsia placed the coffin upon the east steps, the people of Chou placed it on the west steps, the people of Yin placed it between the two pillars. Last night I dreamed that I was sitting before the sacred offerings between the two pillars. Does that mean that I am a man of Yin?

Seven days later Confucius died, being seventy-three years old. The venerable sage was lamented by people who, even though they found his standards too demanding for their own ways of life, admired him for his intelligence, scholarship and probity. He was buried on the banks of the river Szu, and was publicly mourned, his disciples staying for three years at the grave site in an unusual display of grief. At the end of that time most scattered to their homes, but a few remained. Tze Kung built a hut by the grave mound and remained another six years; over a hundred other disciples, with their families, also built huts around the mound, and the site was known as the Hamlet of Confucius. Religious rites began to be celebrated there every year, taking the

form of a banquet and an archery contest. The building where
the disciples had been quartered during the Sage's lifetime was
turned into a temple, which contained his relics—his hat, clothing, lute and chariot. The Confucian cult became an important
one for dignitaries, and the site of his burial mound was routinely
visited and honored by emperors, princes and officials before
attending to mere prosaic business.

More than ten generations after the Sage's death, Sse-ma went
to Lu to visit the temple. "I contemplated his chariot," he wrote,
"his garments, and his ceremonial implements. At a certain time
scholars performed the rites of his house. So I remained there,
full of reverence, and could not tear myself away . . . Even now
his doctrine is still handed down, and men of learning honor him
as Master. From the Son of Heaven [the emperor], and from
kings and princes on, all who practice the six free arts in the
Middle Kingdom take their decisions and their measures from the
Master. That can be designated the highest possible sanctity."

The honors given the Sage were more than those due sanctity
alone. The people saw Confucius not only as a wise and good man
but as a deity. By 174 B.C. pilgrims to his shrine celebrated the
rites with the offerings normally sacrificed for a god. The various
kings, especially of the Han dynasty (206 B.C. to A.D. 220), raised
him higher and higher in their hierarchy of deities until Confucius became equal to the gods of heaven and earth. At the same
time, under the the Han court the magical elements of Tao were
taken up—practices that the old Taoist recluses supposedly engaged in, such as flying through the air, or walking through a
mountainside, or walking under water. These occult practices, of
course, came from a misreading of stories about the Taoist sages.
"Taoist" magic and superstition were combined with the revived
Confucian tenets into a kind of universal faith, which a contemporary Dutch scholar labeled "Chinese Universism," with its

harmony between heaven, earth and man, all the parts and the phenomena of the cosmos being combined together to focus around the ruler, called the T'ien-tse, or Son of Heaven. The Hans made Confucian ideals and tenets the official doctrine of the state, and his teachings were spread to other Asian nations, especially Korea, Japan and the kingdoms of Indochina, where they intermingled with the old nature faiths and the various forms of Buddhism. Confucianism as a state religion ended with the overthrow of the emperor in 1912 and the founding of a republic.

The fate of the great Sage has been clouded since the establishment of the People's Republic of China under the late Mao Tse-tung. Confucius has been denounced from time to time by Mao and his deputies and successors. Yet Confucian ideals of order, probity, dedication to the common good and its hierarchical structure have much in common with practical Marxism. "To make China rich and strong needs several decades of intense effort, which will include, among other things, the effort to practice strict economy and combat waste, i.e., the policy of building up our country through diligence and frugality." For a better China "we . . . must preserve all useful means of production and of livelihood, taking resolute measures against anyone's destroying or wasting them, oppose extravagant eating and drinking and pay attention to thrift and economy." Either sentence could have been said by Confucius were he alive today; actually, Mao stated them. But it would be foolish and unhistorical to pretend that Mao and the Chinese leaders were or are in any sense Confucians; nevertheless, they were conditioned by the all-pervading Confucianism of their childhood, and such conditioning is hard to throw off. Confucius's ideas of a well-structured society, with each person fitting into his or her proper place for the benefit of all, easily slides into Chinese Marxism. A contemporary Chinese scholar, Liu Wu-chi, writes:

Despite the difference in their socio-economic background and the incompatibility of their basic tenets, the teachings of K'ung [that is, Confucius] and Marx are similar in their common concern for the practical, material aspects of life, in the monolithic structure of the two systems, and in the political role played by their partisans.

Even if the People's Republic banned all of the Confucian works they would probably survive in some way. Once previously, almost all works by philosophers and scholars were destroyed in China. In the third century B.C. the remote and backward state of Ch'in began a series of wars against its more advanced and sophisticated neighbors. By 221 B.C. all of China had been unified into one vast state as the result of Ch'in's more powerful armies and political maneuverings, and King Cheng of Ch'in took the crown as the first emperor of China. His prime minister, Li Ssu, in drawing up reforms that would turn the new empire from a feudal society into a totalitarian state, told Cheng that scholars, as supporters of the feudal past, were no longer needed. He suggested to the emperor that "all historical records save those of Ch'in, be burned; that all libraries of poetry, history, and philosophy . . . be destroyed; that all people who recite poetry or discuss history be executed." He also recommended that what was kept be maintained under lock and key, to be administered by a few trusted scholars. Cheng had 460 leading intellectuals buried alive and all suspect works destroyed.

It seemed that the Confucian age was dead, all the writings lost, along with all the other great books of China. But history took one of its accustomed, and we might say, strange and expected turns. A new warrior king appeared. He was Liu Pang, the founder of the great Han dynasty, an illiterate nomad who despised scholars. But he found that the works of Confucius and the other sages had their uses. By the time of his son, the second Eminent Emperor, a fervent attempt was under way to retrieve the great works of the past from the memories of those scholars still alive. Men now ancient—some in their nineties—wrote down what they had recalled from memory; some were able to dig out from hiding places within walls bamboo tablets with some of the revered writings of Confucius.

Confucius always took the long view, drawing upon works as old as five hundred to two thousand years as if they had been written in his childhood. So it seems that a temporary eclipse at the present will hardly affect the long-term devotion of the Chinese people to their greatest Master and Teacher.

5

THE NATURE RELIGIONS: BON AND SHINTO

Since the most primitive ages the forces of nature have charmed, threatened and nurtured mankind. For some, gentle streams, lakes, ponds, rivers, verdant fields, flowery meadows, lush farmlands, unusual formations of rocks and stones, mountains and the rolling skies, the sun and moon, the winds and breezes, the quiet ocean swells, have invoked reverence and prayer. For others, nature can threaten and overwhelm, destroy and avenge. Storms, earthquakes, volcanoes, fierce winds, snow and ice, raging seas, turbulent lakes, rock slides and impassable gorges and inaccessible mountain peaks put nature into a savage perspective, with savage deities to confront. For the thoughtful man, as we have seen in the case of the Jains, nature throbs with divine life, though this faith sees that each particle of matter contains a soul enchained. But other Ways view each natural object as containing a different kind of soul, not one that must be liberated, but one that must, as in the case of the Bon-po of Tibet, be appeased and

feared, or, as with the Shintoists of Japan, be revered and honored. Bon, the faith of the Bon-po, is the indigenous, primitive,
pre-Buddhist religion of that part of Asia which includes not only
Tibet, but western China, Bhutan and Sikkim, though in the
latter lands Bon is less carefully defined and might be called
nothing more descriptive than "the old religion." Shinto is also an
indigenous, primitive pre-Buddhist religion, but unlike Bon,
which views nature with awesome respect, it takes a reverential
view that is more casual, and though certain forces must be
handled with respect (like those of earthquakes and volcanoes),
the attitude is much more positive.

BON

The first king of Tibet, Gna-k'ri-bstan-po, is said to have come
down from heaven by a rope. The rope was called dmu-t'ag. In
some versions of the story it is woven of silver, while in others it is
a golden chain. The rope-chain was depicted on the grave memo-
rials of the royalty. In fact, however, the Tibetans did not believe
that the kings died in the manner of ordinary souls but ascended
to heaven by means of this silver (or gold) link. And this same tie
to heaven served to keep the king in touch with the gods above
during his lifetime. This was the religion of Bon, the indigenous,
pre-Buddhist faith of Tibet. Its members are known as Bon-po,
or, sometimes, Bon-poba. The origin of the term is unknown,
though European scholars believe it to be derived from the mur-
muring of shamans, the Asian sorcerer-magician priests who are
found throughout the eastern sections of the continent and
were — and are — especially powerful in Tibet.

Tibet is a wild, desolate land, a vast, high plateau, often barren
and stony, bordered on the south by the highest mountains in the
world, the Himalayas, and on the other quarters open to trackless
spaces of Asia. Above is that strange sky remarked upon by the
few foreigners who have penetrated these fierce spaces, some-

times empty and pale, sometimes cloud-crammed, a sky that sheds blessings and maledictions impartially upon the land and the people below. Earthquakes, drought, storms, fierce winds, heavy snows, biting cold and burning sun give a special anguish to the sparse life of people and animals. Yet the daring foreigners who have visited the plateau are joined in saying that the Tibetans are a happy people.

In the old days, before the Buddhists came (in the seventh century A.D.) to give a semblance of government, religion and culture to the land, the people were as wild as the plateau and the mountains. Wherever they went, they faced the forces of nature at their most ferocious; everything was known to be inhabited by spirits. Rivers, streams, lakes, rocks, mountains, trees, caves, paths, palaces of the kings and the huts of the peasants, even the hearths, were the abodes of deities. Here and there were places with more powerful gods than others. Mountain passes, paths along sheer cliffs, bridges over deep ravines and streams were especially feared for the power of the deity within. All over Tibet are cairns of rocks to which every passerby — Buddhist as well as Bon-po — adds his own stone as a mark of respect and propitiation.

It was the special province of the shamans to control and subdue the natural deities. These sorcerer-priests possessed great occult strengths, for they had to wrestle with or appease the gods. Long aware that the spirits could take over the body of a person — the ill, the crazy, the dying — the shamans in the early days came to know which rites and rituals could gain superiority over the forces of the other world. Eventually the shamans went even further than face-to-face encounters with the gods and demons. They learned how to absorb the spirits into their own bodies in order to employ the spirits' powers for their own purposes. Forces that had once been enemies now inhabited the physical shells of the shamans. It was a procedure fraught with danger, for the wrong move would expose the shaman to the full fury of the imprisoned spirit, and he would go insane or die.

This stage in Bon was observed by early Chinese travelers, and noted in their writings. A great sacrifice was held every three years, in which donkeys and human beings were offered to the gods of the three regions, Heaven, Earth and the Underworld. Sheep, dogs and monkeys were sacrificed in lesser and less frequent rites. The ritual involved disemboweling the victim and scattering his, or its, blood into the air. The Buddhists tried to stamp out such sacrificial rites by persuading the Bon-po to substitute paper drawings and effigies, but even in this century responsible Buddhists have reported that the rites survive in isolated areas. One of the common homes of spirits was the juniper tree. Its berries, trunk and branches are still offered as sacrifices, and the berries are also used as a narcotic to induce ecstatic trances.

Not only might others be sacrificed, but a Bon-po who had complete control over the demons whom he had taken in as, so to say, a soul-partner, might even immolate himself. As recently as the last century a French missionary named Huc witnessed the manifestation of the powers of a noted lama (the term means merely teacher) called Bokté Rinpoche.

A Lama was to cut himself open, take out his entrails, and place them before him, and then resume his previous condition. This spectacle, so cruel and disgusting, is very common in the lamaseries of Tartary. The Bokté [Lama] who is to manifest his power . . . prepares himself for the formidable operation by many days' fasting and prayer, pending which he must abstain from all communication whatever with mankind, and must observe the most absolute silence. When the appointed day is come, the multitude of pilgrims assemble in the great court of the lamasery, where an altar is raised in front of the temple gate. At length the Bokté appears. He advances gravely, amid the acclamation of the crowd, seats himself upon the altar and takes from his belt a large knife which he places upon his knees. At his feet numerous lamas, ranged in a circle, commence the terrible invocations of this frightful ceremony. As the recitation of prayers proceeds, you see the Bokté trembling in every limb, and gradually working himself up into phrenetic convulsions. The lamas themselves become excited; their voices are raised; their song follows no order, and at last becomes a confusion of yelling and outcry. Then the Bokté suddenly throws aside the shawl which envelops him, unfastens his belt, and, seizing the sacred knife, slits open his stomach in one long cut. While the blood flows in every direction, the multitude prostrate themselves before the terrible spectacle, and the enthusiast is questioned about all sorts of hidden things, as to future events, as to the destiny of certain individuals. The replies of the Bokté to all these questions are regarded by everybody as oracles.

When the devout curiosity of the numerous pilgrimages is satisfied, the lamas resume, but now calmly and gravely, the recitation of their prayers. The Bokté takes in his right hand blood from his wound, raises it to his mouth, breathes thrice upon it, then throws it into the air with loud cries. He next passes his hand rapidly over his wound, closes it, and everything after a while resumes its former condition, no trace remaining of the diabolical operation except extreme prostration. The Bokté again winds his shawl around him, recites a short prayer in a low voice; then all is over and the multitude disperse, except for a few of the exceptionally devout who remain to contemplate and adore the blood-stained altar which the saint has left.

Calm reflection will tell us that Bokté was deceiving his followers, but Abbé Huc states that "we do not believe that there is any trick or deception about [such ceremonies]; for, from all we have seen and heard among idolatrous nations, we are persuaded that the devil has a great deal to do with the matter; moreover, our impression that there is no trick in the operation is supported by the opinion of the most intelligent and most upright Buddhists we have met in the numerous lamaseries we have visited."

What early Bon was like is known from the few descriptions of foreigners — Chinese, Indians, Nepalese — who entered the land either as missionaries or travelers and businessmen, or from the analysis of Tibetan Buddhist material, for it is saturated by Bon. However, Bon after the Buddhist invasion became markedly Buddhist in certain aspects, though, of course, the two faiths are distinct and in the past were often at war with each other. Bon changed noticeably after the seventh century, and with the backward projection of later ideas, both Bon and Buddhist, there is some confusion about what the Bon-po actually believe. They know that there is a heavenly deity, a celestial king or overlord, who stands above but does not interfere with the affairs of the world. He resides in Pagopunsum, a sacred mountain peak, eighteen thousand feet high, in northeastern Tibet, surrounded by his ministers, who live in lesser peaks. Two tutelary spirits live among men, communication with them being achieved by the shamans while in an ecstatic trance. There was also a cult of warrior gods and many minor gods and spirits to whom sacrifices, often of humans, had to be made. The early kings, connected to heaven by their silver or gold cords and chains, were divine. Eventually, as Bon entered more sophisticated stages, the cord had to be cut, and from then on the royalty was entombed in great burial mounds along with their faithful retainers and various possessions.

Tibet served as a crossroads for caravans passing along an east-west axis between China and lands such as Iran and the Middle East. The legendary founder of Bon. Mi-bo gshen-rab, was believed to have been born in a Zoroastrian area, possibly Iran itself but more likely (if there is any fact in the story) in what is now southern Russia. Some Zoroastrian elements have been found in Bon; yet they may be but coincidences. In the later Bon and Buddhist texts, Mi-bo gshen-rab bears a strong resemblance to Gautama Buddha, symbolizing the effort of the Buddhist missionaries to adapt indigenous beliefs to their own Way rather than crushing them. The unique characteristics of Bon as an independent faith have been swallowed by Buddhism, and where the primordial sect is found today (if at all, due to the Chinese occupation) it is in the northern and eastern border regions where there was less proselytizing from India.

In absorbing Bon, or parts of it, Tibetan Buddhism took over a number of shamanistic elements. Among them we find practices like magical flight, and the ascent to heaven by means of a ladder or rope (as in the case of the early Tibetan kings), practices which are documented in Bon-po tradition. The famous *Tibetan Book of the Dead*, the Bardo Thodol, according to the editor-translator W. Y. Evans-Wentz is largely of Bon origin. The work deals with the ancient problem of the dead not knowing that they are dead, disembodied spirits that are simply continuing their earthly existence, and gives instructions in living the life beyond without having to experience the cycle of birth and rebirth. The making of effigies of the dead is a Bon rather than a Buddhist custom, says Evans-Wentz, and he traces it back to an origin held in common with the funeral rites of ancient Egypt. The Bon-po originally were formed in clans with animal totems, which survive today in the form of the animal masks worn by Tibetan-Buddhist priests in various rituals or in mystery plays of great antiquity. In this use, the animals are symbols of sagsaric, or embodied, beings — human, subhuman and superhuman. Like many of the shamanist peoples of Asia, the Bon believed in a primitive form of rebirth; thus, when the Buddhists arrived to preach a similar doctrine, though in more complex terms, many Bon-po accepted Buddhism as a fulfillment of their own Way. The influence of the Buddhists gradually brought the Bon-po to a reorganization of their own religion. Temples and later monasteries were constructed along Buddhist forms. The art of writing, introduced by the foreign missionaries, brought a great surge of learning among the Bon-po, and a Bon literature of great prolixity and complexity, much of it akin to that of Buddhism but with Bon terminology.

Today the Bon superficially resemble the Buddhists, yet Tibetan Buddhists are careful to point out that Bon is quite separate from the Way of the Buddha, for the Bon-po do not recognize Gautama Buddha. One gains the sense that the wild, primitive, archaic ways of ancient Tibet, of Bon Tibet, still survive in strength and that the Buddhists still fear them. A noted Tibetan Buddhist, Thubten Jigme Norbu, recognized as the reincarnation of the fifteenth-century Tibetan lama Tagster (and also the older brother of the Dalai Lama), states in summary of the Bon-po:

> They too are striving for liberation, but they are impatient for it. They seek short cuts and they seek to escape the results of their deeds. They play with powers which they claim to exist outside their bodies but which we hold to be of no concern to us. Sometimes they only achieve their own destruction, but who is to deny that sometimes they too achieve liberation.

The state of the Bon-po today is unknown, for Tibet is an occupied country and the invaders have done everything to wipe out the past and to impose a socialist economy. In 1950 troops of the Chinese People's Republic occupied Tibet, only a year after the successful Communist victory in China itself. At first the Tibetans were told by the Chinese that they could continue as before, with their Buddhist god-king, the Dalai Lama, still ruling. But land reforms started by the Chinese soon undermined the powerful, feudal strengths of the monasteries. Peasant revolts broke out, followed by a nationwide rebellion in 1959. The Dalai Lama and many of the higher monks and thousands of the laity fled to India. Many Tibetans were reported killed by the Chinese, or starved to death or resettled in other parts of China. Bon, which had existed in a shadowy world of its own, had no spokesmen to ask the world for help as the Tibetan Buddhists, with their many exiles abroad, could. But as we know, old ideas, traditional ways, often survive under the most difficult conditions. Bon, though under extreme pressure from Buddhism in the past, was able to retain much of its integrity and was even able to influence its conquerors. What happens to Bon — and to Tibetan Buddhism too — in the Tibetan Autonomous Region of China (as the ancient plateau is now called) will be a matter for history.

SHINTO

On February 11, 660 B.C. — we know the date because it has been recorded in the eighth-century A.D. work, the Record of Ancient Things (or *Kojiki*) — Jimmu-Tenno, the Emperor of the Godly Warriors, led his tribe into Yamato on the great island of Honshu off the eastern coast of Asia. Jimmu-Tenno was a descendent of the sun goddess Amaterasu-o-mi-Kami, literally the Heavenly Shining Great August Deity, via her grandson Ninigi-no-Mikete, who had received from her the symbols of empire — the mirror, sword and jewels still used as the royal insignia of the ruling house of Japan. Since that time the goddess's descendants have ruled the country in an unbroken line, all the rulers being considered of divine status. It was not until the end of World War II that the emperor Hirohito renounced all claims to heavenly descent and became a mere mortal like any of his common subjects.

Amaterasu is the greatest of all Japanese deities. She produced the rice fields, the canals to irrigate them, and organized the rituals and ceremonies, especially those dealing with purity. Among the ancient inhabitants of Japan, and among many today, the great sin was not an act of crime but a neglect of the rites to ensure perfection and purity in all aspects of worship and life.

The origins of Japan are clouded in the mists of primordial time. Shinto (the name means the Way of the Gods), the ancient religion, had no written literature, and much of value was lost during the period before the arrival of the Buddhists during the sixth century A.D. Up to then virtually everything was transmitted orally, the only notable exceptions being some codes of law.

When the Chinese came to bring Buddhism to Japan, much as the Indians did to Tibet, they began to assemble and edit the mass of oral tradition. Two great collections of ancient Shinto history were made—even the name Shinto did not exist until about the Chinese period. The *Kojiki* and the *Nihon-shoki*, or *Nihongi* (Chronicles of Japan), show strong Chinese and Korean influences.

The histories do not agree in the details of the origin of the cosmos or of the islands. The *Nihongi* states a cosmogonic theory in which Heaven and Earth came from an egg-shaped mass. Included in this is a theogonic theory, which tells of seven generations of gods, ending with two who are central figures in Shinto, Izanagi and his wife Izanami—the male who invites and the female who invites. The other heavenly deities ordered them to descend to earth to produce the terrestrial world, beginning with the fields of Japan, then the forms of nature, the waters, winds, mountains, meadows, food, fire and mist. Their final act was the creation of the rulers of the world, of whom the Sun Goddess Amaterasu was paramount. The *Kojiki* version is somewhat different. Izanagi and Izanami stirred the formless mass that had come out of the cosmic chaos with a jeweled spear, from the point of which fell a drop of matter that became an island. The two deities descended to the island, were married, and gave birth to eight other islands, and lastly to Amaterasu.

Whatever the version, the Sun Goddess remains the greatest of all spirits. She did not have an easy time of it, though; her brother, the Moon God, mistreated her so badly that she was forced to hide in a cave, but the loss of her beneficial rays brought the other deities to beg her to return to her usual place. Her shrine is located at Ise in southwest Honshu, and is the most important pilgrimage center of the Japanese archipelago. Amaterasu's cult was originally celebrated in the royal palace but was later transferred to Ise, to be served by the princes. The move made her worship open to the public, instead of keeping it as

[117]

a private cult of the emperor. The shift was as much political as religious, for it helped focus the people's devotion and loyalty on the ruler as the descendant and heir of the goddess. Soon the cult became so popular that most Japanese, no matter what other religious loyalties they may have had (such as to the various sects of Buddhism), made the pilgrimage at least once in a lifetime.

The shrine consists of a number of wooden buildings located in a dense forest near the Isuzu River. A series of four fences, one within the other, encloses the central shrine, the shoden. Within the shoden is the sacred mirror in which Amaterasu's spirit resides. Only the emperor and the priests may enter the shoden. But around it are other buildings — numerous small shrines and pavilions for pilgrims. The entire shrine undergoes a curious ritual of rebirth every twenty years. Ever since the seventh century A.D. the entire structure, from the fences to the shoden, has been rebuilt on an identical neighboring site in order to renew the symbolic youth and purity of Shinto.

When the new shrine is completed, the mirror with its spirit of Amaterasu is led from the old shoden (which is taken down and cut into chips for the pilgrims) to the new shrine of the Rich Food Goddess, one of the attendant deities at Ise, to receive offerings of food, and then it is installed in the new shoden in a ritual of consecration. The rite should be repeated next in 1994, but there are fears that the most recent rebuilding, in 1974, was the last, for the tradition of the skilled woodworker and craftsman in Japan is dying out, and probably there will be no one left capable of the necessary detailed and elaborate carpentry for the shrine, the TV assembly line having replaced the traditional woodworker's shop.

Besides the major deities, such as the Sun Goddess and the Rich Food Goddess, there is a myriad of spirits in Shinto called kami. How many kami there are is not clearly established. The word originally meant "upper," and was probably associated with the

At the Shinto center at Ise, the inner shrine, the Kotai-jingu, is sacred to the sun goddess, Amaterasu. The Kotai-jingu contains the mirror enshrining the soul of the Goddess. The building is renewed every twenty years in an exact duplicate on an adjoining site. The form of the shrine, with its cross beams on top and exposed rafters, goes back to archaic times.

thousands of spirits who dwelt in the peaks of sacred mountains and condescended to visit the earth from time to time, especially if wooed by music and efficacious rites. The kami include such important deities as those of the moon, the planets, the storms and the sea, fire, food and rice, to name but a few, plus those of minor importance, such as those of the parts of a house, the door, kitchen, hearth, privy and so on. Twelve emperors are also honored as deities.

The kami inhabit not only fields and crops, but also forests, trees, rocks, mountains and islands. One of their favorite dwelling places is an object known as the yorishiro, which might be a tree of an unusual shape, or an elongated rock of marked characteristics. (Kami will also take up residence in man-made objects, such as dolls or wands, or flags and swords.) A twisted tree outlined against the horizon, or a stone of unusual shape, by reason of its uniqueness is obviously the home of kami descended to earth. And such unexpected forms as the cone of Mount Fuji or an island washed by ocean tides and winds might also be the dwelling places of kami. Many natural sites became shrines, sanctified because spirits lived within them. Whether or not Japanese of more sophistication believe in the actual presence of kami in their gardens or in the forests and along the seacoasts, the special awe that a beautiful site can bring instills even in them a reverence for nature that is peculiarly Japanese.

Worship of the kami includes various rituals, among them sacrifices of rice and rice cakes and rice wine, or sake. Sacrifices of animals and humans have long since died out, and the average Japanese would be astonished to know that his ancestors practiced them, though effigies are sometimes used today. Worship may take place in a private home or originate in the home and be completed in a shrine, the miya (ya, meaning house, plus the honorific mi). Japan has a profuse number of miya, usually simple wooden buildings consisting of a prayer hall and a central hall. In the distant past worship seems to have been celebrated in the open before whatever rocks, trees or bodies of water (or even the sun) contained the presence of the god. Later, worship was brought indoors.

At the miya, prayer is conducted by the priest, who stands inside the building, while the people remain outside. Originally worship consisted of obeisance, various offerings, prayers and petitions. Later there developed the custom of the gohei, an implement consisting of strips of cloth attached to a stick and placed upon the altar. The gohei came to be considered as sanctified in itself and to contain the deity mystically descended. Today gohei may be made of mulberry-bark paper, or, in another form called nusa, of paper on a hempen rope, and suspended from the rafters. Both gohei and nusa confer a special sanctity wherever they might be enshrined.

Many Japanese consider themselves both Shintoists and Buddhists. In fact, it would be difficult to get the average person to express a preference for one Way or the other. Association with the Shinto Way begins about thirty days after birth for the Japanese child, who is brought to a local Shinto shrine to be presented to the deities. The child is now known as an ujiko, or child of the kami of the particular area, and throughout his life remains attached to that deity. The association is seen as a kind of parent-child relationship, one which is found throughout the Japanese social structure, not only in family life but even in business, where the management or the boss takes on a parental role for the workers, no matter how skilled, professional or old they may be. The ujiko visits his Shinto shrine from time to time—though he may have moved to another area—to let the gods know of changes in life (marriage, perhaps a new job, some honor, a birth in the family), to request success in a college examination or to pray for good health, or merely to pray without any special purpose except that of thanks and well-being. Until the post-war period this familial relationship extended not only through the gods of one's shrine but even to the emperor himself, the divine descendant of Amaterasu.

This calm relationship with the kami has not always been an easy one, for Buddhism did much harm to Shinto, and until slightly more than a century ago, when the royal house regained its powers, Shinto had been pushed into the role of a second-class faith by the Buddhists. The earliest accounts of Shinto are found in various Chinese-language chronicles of the eighth century A.D. and later. In these works three different types of priests are mentioned: the Imibe, whose responsibility was to maintain the ritual purity of the people and of objects connected with ceremonies; the Nakatomi, a clan, who enjoyed the power of communicating with the gods on behalf of the emperor and who performed the liturgies and the rites, and the Urabe, who were diviners and had the customary powers of seeking out the future or of interpreting events. These three groups — called "corporations" in the translations — had the exclusive privilege of dealing directly with the gods. A fourth class, a priestly caste, who lived as laymen (often as government officials), discharged various religious duties.

The earliest stages of Shinto can only be surmised from what was written later, after the introduction of Buddhism into Japan in A.D. 552. What has survived are some great burial mounds of the princes, numerous clay figures called haniwa, which may have been meant as substitutions for human sacrifices, clay models of shrines, a few mirrors, bells and other implements. The early Shinto teachings, as reported by the Chinese Buddhists, depicted the universe as being neither friendly nor hostile. Divinity was manifest in everything. There was a concept of the soul, which existed in two parts, one mild-mannered, cheerful and linked to health and prosperity, and one the opposite, sometimes associated with evil, and impetuous and adventurous. The soul was a substance, a pale ball of fire which could be discerned in the darkness after an individual's death. It became a spirit, a kami, or even a major divinity if the personage were important. The chronicles indicate that there were no standard forms of belief, for the primitive Shintoism comprised many varied cults among the different clans and tribes of the scattered archipelago.

After the sixth century, when Shinto and Buddhism met head-on, more precise information was recorded about the local cults. However, the indigenous beliefs were being interpreted in terms of the more sophisticated Chinese thought and culture of the missionaries. Foreign ideas, not only from Buddhism (which, of course, was originally Indian) but from Confucianism and Taoism as well, influenced Shinto, for many Chinese and Koreans were flocking to the islands, among them monks and mystics, businessmen and soldiers, and numerous craftsmen, all of whom brought not only alien ways but alien religious concepts. Buddhism swallowed Shinto whole, though the two extremes of the nation, the royal court and the peasants, retained their Shintoism more or less pure. The warrior class, the businessmen and traders, the middle class and the well-to-do landowners were the great supporters of Buddhism. Shinto had no philosophy to support itself, and little organization. After the initial impact, in which Buddhist temples drove away the Shinto gods, or absorbed them as forms of Buddhist deities, Shinto reached the point where statues of the Buddha himself were found in most Shinto shrines. Shinto had become an inferior form of Buddhism. Even the emperor, who owed direct allegiance to the Sun Goddess, Amaterasu, was forced to compromise, and to accept her as an aspect of the Buddha.

After the ninth century A.D. the shoguns (literally, "throne field marshals"), the military dictators who opposed the royal family, isolated the emperor and Shinto, though the emperor remained sacred. Some Confucian doctrines crept in after the 1600s to assert the role of the emperor as the divine father of the nation, acknowledging his descent in an unbroken line from Amaterasu. Meanwhile the populace could both attend Buddhist ceremonies and follow Shinto customs without having to make a choice of one or the other, for the ancient faith was still a vivifying force among the ordinary people. The revival of Shinto came in 1868, when some of the samurai, the warrior aristocrats, shifted their allegiance from the shoguns to the emperor, forcing the resignation of the current and last dictator. With the emperor as the fixed point of both religious and political life, Shinto and the state reinforced each other's strengths and Buddhism became a lesser power. Shinto was now the official embodiment of the national spirit of Japan, a role it maintained until Hirohito publicly renounced his divinity in his New Year message of 1946. This step may have pleased the occupying Americans, but many ordinary Japanese who practiced Shinto saw little significance in the move, for Amaterasu still shone upon the land of the Rising Sun.

Today Shinto still is an active force in Japan but is heavily influenced by its rival, Buddhism. Much of Shinto philosophy has been absorbed from Buddhism. Efforts have been made to purify Shintoism, but both faiths still tend to meld together, for they have become so entwined over the centuries and so much a part of the Japanese heart and soul that a clear-cut break would be a psychological disaster. In this century a number of minor Shinto cults have arisen — some in reaction to Buddhist influences — stressing different aspects of the ancestral faith and even of other religions. Some sects attempt to return to archaic sources; others have turned to nationalism. Some groups preach a single God in place of the myriad deities of the past, and others a Trinity which parallels that of Christianity. Still others, influenced by Zen, now stress such practices as yoga and faith healing. Attempts by the Japanese government to take true census counts of Shintoists and Buddhists have been frustrated, for the majority of the people of the archipelago claim allegiance to both Ways.

[124]

A Shinto wedding combines a mixture of styles and forms. The priest wears a traditional cap and robes and carries a scepter, symbolic of his position. The accompanying monks are dressed in Buddhist robes. The bride wears the ceremonial kimono and a head-dress called the tsunokakushi, sign of her obedience to her future husband. The groom is dressed in western morning clothes, a style made popular by the emperors since the nineteenth century. Today, a movement called Tenchakuren ("League to Dress the Emperor") is trying to persuade Hirohito, the current ruler, and the symbol and embodiment of Shinto, to return to traditional Japanese dress, and to speak correct Japanese.

SOME "NEW" RELIGIONS:
CAO DAI, THE BAHA'I FAITH
THEOSOPHY

The religious yearning in mankind is always present. One may attack religion, ridicule it, modernize it to the point of extinction; governments may legislate against it, suppress it, stamp it out, martyr the faithful—yet somehow, somewhere else, religious beliefs appear again, as a restless mankind tries to come to terms with the self, the soul, the environment and the cosmos. Times change and so do religious faiths and beliefs: some develop and mature, others wither away. Sometimes one wonders if all religions are not actually expressing the same Ground of All Being, or, diversely, if they are not but various Paths to the same Summit, differentiated by culture and history. In the end one has to face the fact that even against the greatest odds humanity will seek out some way of joining its small individual sparks of life to the great Sun of the cosmos.

For thousands of years five great religions—Hinduism, Buddhism, Judaism, Islam and Christianity—have been serving the world, as have the lesser faiths described in the previous chapters of this volume. Yet prophets and saints, innovators, reformers and adapters arise to claim that the five great faiths are still but partial realizations of the Truth. Thus we can see that the three small movements described in this chapter fulfill some inherent need. All three profess to be "world" religions (and perhaps they may be someday, though one's intuitions say otherwise), supplementing the earlier faiths. Each professes to be the Answer to the world's problems, both religious and secular. The Baha'i Faith (named after its founder Baha'Allah) sprang from the messianic expectations of a savior; Cao Dai (Reigning God) developed as a Way of uniting the best of the major religions, without their faults; and Theosophy (which translates as the "knowledge of the divine") sees the world dependent on the incarnations of a series of Buddha forms who will save the world. There are others similar to these three which I have selected because they are both unusual and typical, and symbolize the unquenchable flame within the human soul.

CAO DAI

In the period immediately after World War I, in the French colony of Indochina, a rather corrupt and unpleasant man named Ngo-van-Chieu had taken up the practice of spiritualism, using attractive young women as his mediums. Ngo-van-Chieu was from Annam, one of the many nations in the southeast Asian peninsula, and a minor official in the French colonial government. At a session in 1919, the spirit of Cao Dai (Reigning God, as Ngo translated it) appeared, and a divine voice ordered him to proclaim a new doctrine to the people of the Indo-Chinese peninsula. In Saigon, in 1925, Ngo-van-Chieu had a second vision, this one in the presence of a number of minor government officials. Among the group was a notorious businessman, Le-van-Trung, an opium addict and lecher. Le was on the brink of financial ruin

[127]

because of dishonest business practices, and his creditors and the police were about to move against him. Le-van-Trung was so affected by Ngo's vision that he changed his way of life and became a member of the Cao Dai movement. The founder soon retired and left his disciple, the reformed crook, to take over. Under Le's aegis Cao Dai flourished and soon became popular throughout Indochina.

Cao Dai—which can mean High Place as well as Reigning God—was the name given to both the movement and the leading deity. The full title of the cult is Dai Dao Tam Pho Do. It signifies the Third Pardon of God and is the central tenet of the faith, being a fulfillment of the two previous pardons, those of the West (Judaism and Christianity) and of the East (Taoism, Confucianism and Buddhism), none of which the Cao Daists saw as complete for mankind. Cao Dai is symbolized by the Eye of God, surrounded by rays signifying the omniscience and universality of the Almighty overlooking the world.

Though the movement was new and syncretist—that is, it was formed from many sources—it had roots going back to very early times in the history of the peninsula. The area had long been the target of invaders from two very powerful lands, India on its west and China to its north. Buddhist missionaries had probably come to the land in the third century B.C. under the auspices of the Indian emperor Ashoka. Then many Hindus, as well as Buddhists, came to trade and to find kingdoms, for some of the warrior princes from as far away as Gujarat on India's northwestern coast invaded the land to seek their fortunes and stayed as rulers. By the second century A.D. there were Indian kingdoms in the remotest parts of the peninsula. Indians founded the kingdom of Kambuja, later called Cambodia. The first ruler, Kaundinya, is credited with introducing the elements of civilization; also he "taught the people to wear clothes." Indian concepts—both Hindu and Buddhist—infiltrated everywhere, and Indian religion, culture and societal forms became dominant. Even today the great Hindu epics, the *Ramayana* and the *Mahabharata,* form the core of the land's civilization. Meanwhile the Chinese, too, were interested in the peninsula, and from the beginning of the second century A.D. to A.D. 939 most of what is now Vietnam (the sections known previously as Tonkin and Annam) were incorporated into the Chinese empire. The Chinese introduced Confucianism and Taoism and forms of Buddhism which resembled Zen. The Annamese and Tonkinese themselves, in their primitive stages, followed various animistic cults. In the nineteenth century the French took over most of the peninsula, except for Thailand on the west, and brought with them Roman Catholicism. Soon the Indo-Chinese people were split, roughly, between those who were Christians and those who followed various forms of Buddhism, especially the mystical path called Thien (which was a version of the Chinese sect known as Ch'an in the mainland and Zen in Japan). But Buddhism was influenced by Taoism, Confucianism and animism. The Vietnamese at times tried to purge their land of foreign faiths, especially Buddhism. What the Christians did was also of concern, but the masters, the French, were Christian, and anti-Catholic sentiments were carefully kept private.

But Cao Dai, or the young women who served to interpret His messages to Ngo-van-Chieu and Le-van-Trung, had a different approach. The two men, the founder and his disciple, met the matter of foreign religions in what they thought was a more positive manner. Instead of rejecting the other faiths wholeheartedly, they took what they thought was best in them. Thus Cao Dai — His rays shining over the entire world — contains the best of the world's teachings. Cao Dai doctrine is drawn from five major sources: the animism and spiritualism of the people — both indigenous practices of long standing — and Confucianism, Taoism, Buddhism and Catholicism. With the exception of Islam and Judaism, two faiths he may have had very little acquaintance with, Ngo-van-Chieu had spanned man's religious history, experience and knowledge. These five faiths (animism and spiritualism being counted as one) are the Five Branches of the Cao Dai Great Path leading to perfection.

Through Moses and Jesus in the West, and Lao Tzu and Buddha Sakyamuni in the East, God has already remitted the sins of mankind. These figures are all incarnations of God as man. But now in Cao Dai, God remains as Pure Spirit, the Third Pardon, the form in which He appeared to Ngo-van-Chieu. His message is universal, being one of "love, life and truth" as found in all religions, which are now to be united in the Dai Dao Tam Pho Do. In the Cao Dai cathedral in Saigon, images of Confucius, Jesus, Lao Tzu, Buddha, Joan of Arc and Victor Hugo appear with numerous representations of the Divine Eye. Hugo is included because he is known to have been a spiritualist.

Central authority is held in the members of the Cun Trug Dai, a ruling body which is headed by the Supreme Pontiff, Giao Tong. However, since the death of Le-van-Trung, the Giao Tong has not been a living person but the spirit of the ancient Vietnamese poet-sage Thai Bach, who was represented on earth by Le-van-Trung. The ecclesiastical structure closely resembles that of Roman Catholicism, with cardinals, archbishops, priests and seminarians — any of whom may be a man or a woman. Cao Dai religious practices are somewhat flexible, taking whatever forms the founders thought opportune.

The members are enjoined to pray four times a day. There are many feast days, celebrated with great élan. Services can be elaborate, since they draw upon the rites and rituals of the great faiths as well as the folk practices of the village people. Various forms of sacrifices are offered, conducted either by priests or priestesses. Mediums play an important role today as in the beginning, their messages being transmitted from various spirits, among them Sun Yat Sen (the first president of the Chinese

Cao Dai contains strong elements of Roman Catholicism in its forms of worship—as in this celebration of a "Mass"—but it is essentially an oriental faith, though with universal yearnings. The men and women are separated in worship, and sit on the ground to pray. Cao Dai doctrines rely heavily upon Confucianism and Indo-Chinese spiritism and animism.

Republic), the Chinese poet Lin Po, Joan of Arc and Victor Hugo. The mediums, in a state of trance, receive the messages in a basket, and then write them down with a pen kept in a basket.

Exemplifying its varied sources, Cao Dai teaches the transmigration of souls, the brotherhood of mankind and kindness to animals and plants, for they, too, are part of the divine plan. Cao Dai also teaches social justice of the type promoted by Christian missionaries, and compulsory schooling. At one time it had a private army of some thirty-five thousand men, who were active in the struggle against both the French in the colonial period and the Vietminh after Indochina was made independent in 1946. At its peak in the 1940s, Cao Dai had over two million members not only in Vietnam but also in the neighboring Indochinese lands of Laos and Cambodia.

Though this movement sought to unify mankind under the banner of the world's greatest religions, it was not free from problems. Le-van-Trung "disincarnated" himself in 1934, at a time when the sect had only three hundred thousand members and was under pressure by the French because of its nationalistic aspirations. But the founder's death did not slow the rapid growth of Cao Dai, though the French tried to get rid of the leaders. They exiled one of them, Prince Cuaom De, who took refuge in Japan, and arrested the top prewar leader Grand Master Truc and his closest associates and sent them to Madagascar. There are in Cao Dai strong millennial elements, that is, yearnings and expectations for a future perfect state on earth. A millennial movement called Tien Thien believed that Prince Cuaom De was a messiah who would liberate them from the French and agitated for his return. World War II was beginning and another movement within Cao Dai, the White Hats, welcomed Japanese intervention. The invading Japanese were hailed as liberators, but soon the Cao Dai, like others in Asia, learned that Japan's plan for a Greater East Asia would not benefit them, and they turned against their allies. The White Hats became the basis for the Cao Dai army which, along with other Indo-Chinese, fought the French. Cao Dai leaders attempted to mediate the quarrels between the Vietminh and South Vietnam at the time of independence, seeking a middle ground, but at one point found themselves fighting both. Though the sect helped Indochina transform a feudal structure and colonial rule into a small group of modern nations, the various peoples' states of the peninsula show little favor to the Cao Dai, and its present status is not known.

THE BAHA'I FAITH

The Prophet Muhammad's cousin and son-in-law Ali is commonly known as the first person to accept the call to Islam, that is, to submission to God, Allah. Ali married Muhammad's daughter Fatima, and eventually was elected the fourth khalif, or leader of the young Islamic community. But the Muslims were divided over his leadership, some of them refusing to recognize his right to be khalif. Ali submitted to arbitration, with the Qur'an as the supreme judge, and was forced to renounce his claim. But the faction which supported him, the Shi'a, refused to abandon their belief that he was a righteous khalif. Thus began, at almost the beginning of the religion's history, the major split within Islam which has existed to the present. The situation became even more fraught with complications when some of the Shi'a turned against Ali and assassinated him in 661. Since then Ali has been known as one of the great martyrs of Islam, and among the Shi'a the day of his death is mourned with special sadness and much emotion. His sons Hasan and Husayn were also murdered, and their deaths, too, are commemorated yearly with much pageantry, emotion and mystical release among the Shi'a, who include some of the poorest people of the Islamic world, their daily lives being epiphanies of suffering and of hopes for redemption.

[133]

The Shi'a soon split further into other sects. The more orthodox Sunnis, the larger movement of Islam, are much more legalistic and scholarly than the Shi'a, and focus their beliefs solely on Muhammad as the culmination of Prophethood, believing he is the last of the messengers God has sent to the world. In contrast, the Shi'a believed that either Ali, or some other messianic figure would return to save the world and to lead the faithful into better times, either on earth or in heaven. The doctrine of the Hidden Imam, or spiritual leader, arose among many sects, some of whom were identified by their chiliastic hopes. Thus there is a Shi'a group known as the Twelvers, who believe in a line of twelve imams after Ali, the last one being a holy man who disappeared mysteriously in the tenth century but who will return. The Seveners have a similar doctrine but a lesser number of imams, and there are other groups who also expect the return, or the appearance of a hidden imam.

The Shi'a Muslims believe that their imams are both sinless and absolutely infallible, a doctrine the Sunnis firmly reject. Not only are the Shi'a imams infallible in dogma and worship but in secular matters as well, and many of them became powerful political leaders. The imam may have almost literal powers of life and death over his people, and it is only in modern times that such authority is being challenged by the faithful. In early times, Persian and Afghan Shi'a sects advanced the concept of the Hidden Imam as the epiphany of the Primeval Light, who is to come to earth to save mankind. A few extremists see the imam as the incarnation of God—Allah—and others as God Himself. So throughout the ages, all across the Middle East, wherever there were Shi'a sects, there were people awaiting the return of their divine teacher and master, and there were men who thought that they themselves had been appointed to be the Hidden Imam in person, descended or returned to earth to lead the people into a land of milk and honey and to free them from their earthly masters.

In the 1840s a young man named Ali Muhammad—note the names of the martyred khalif and the Prophet together—made a tour of the holy cities of Persia and then Arabia, where his religious enthusiasms were stirred to a state reaching mystical trance. Upon his return to his home city of Shiraz in Persia, Ali Muhammad, now twenty-four, assumed the title of Bab and began to preach his own particular Way. He had come at a crucial time among his own sect of Shi'a, the Imami, who took the concept of Bab, the Gateway of Divine Revelation, to denote a stage of self-propulsion in the manifesting of the Divine Being. The cult had reached powerful proportions in the early nineteenth century, and Ali Muhammad saw himself as the incarnation of the Bab, the mystical Gateway. He was a member of the Prophet's family, a siyyid (or sayed, in some spellings), had married at the age of twenty-two and had a son who was born and died during the year he announced his mission to the world. He attracted a small number of disciples—the first eighteen, with the Bab himself as the nineteenth, were known as the Letters of the Living—who saw in his teachings escape from the domination of the mullahs, the Shi'a clergy, who were notorious oppressors of the people. The Bab's claim was easily accepted, too, by the people around him. He soon stated that he was the Midhi, or mahdi, whose coming the Prophet Muhammad had foretold, and he was identified by the Shi'as as the Twelfth Imam (coincidentally named Muhammad) who had disappeared from the sight of mankind in the tenth century. His followers were now known as Babis; they accepted their leader as the Promised One, whose glory was not earthly but spiritual.

Ali Muhammad, as Bab, besides claiming mahdihood, also adopted the sacred title of Nuqtiiula, which means Primal Point, a title applied mystically to Muhammad himself. In doing this, the Bab claimed to rank along with the Prophet in the series of great founders of religion, whereupon the Shi'a priests, the mullahs, declared the Bab an impostor, and began to agitate against him. But the movement continued to grow, and thousands of people joined. The Bab announced also a new calendar, dating it from 1844, the year in which he had discovered himself as the Twelfth Imam, and restoring the old solar year of the Zoroastrians. His other views were eclectic, drawing upon various faiths as he knew them, but leaning heavily towards a form of mysticism that included many deities. He borrowed concepts of good and evil from Zoroastrianism, the doctrines of which had remained among many Persians, especially among the Sufic brotherhoods. His other teachings were of a rather high moral level; one of his notable steps was the very liberal one of announcing the emancipation of women, this in a society where women were kept segregated in harems.

The conflicts with the mullahs became physical; bloody riots took place, and the Bab was arrested and taken to Tabriz, where the governor ordered him and a disciple to be shot. On July 9, 1850 the Bab and his companion were hoisted on ropes to hang outside the prison wall; a squad of soldiers fired at both men. The disciple died immediately, but the Bab's ropes were cut by the bullets and he fell to the ground unhurt. Unfortunately, the Bab lacked the wit to proclaim that he had been saved by divine intervention and so escape death. He was again hoisted to the wall. The soldiers refused to shoot again, so a second squad was needed to complete the execution. His remains were thrown into a moat, but later disciples rescued them and eventually they were brought to the Holy Land (as dear to Muslims as to Jews and Christians) and entombed not far from the cave of Elijah. In the persecutions that followed, many Babis died the most gruesome deaths, an estimated twenty thousand of them being massacred by the government.

The movement continued to survive, despite persecution. One of the Bab's teachings, according to the Baha'i Faith, the religion that eventually developed out of Babism, was that "God would soon 'make manifest' a World Teacher to unite men and women and usher in an age of peace." Among the Babis were two half-brothers, Subh-i-Azal and Baha'Allah (Baha'u'llah, in Baha'i spelling), who determined to carry on the Bab's work. The first brother maintained the doctrines intact, but his sect, the Azalis, are few in number. However, Baha'Allah, drawing upon other sources, proclaimed a new universalist faith, independent of Islam and open to all people of whatever social class.

Baha'Allah, claiming to be the chosen "Manifestation of God" for his age, called upon people to unite, stating that only one common faith and one order could bring an enduring peace to the world. He foresaw that terrible wars would sweep the face of the earth and destroy the institutions and ideas that keep mankind from its rightful unity. His mystical view of himself also made a deep impression on the ordinary Persians, so long accustomed to the expectation of a savior — the Hidden Imam — to rescue them from their daily misery. Baha'Allah stated plainly and repeatedly that he was the long-expected educator and teacher of all peoples, the channel of wondrous Grace that would transcend all previous outpourings of faith, in which all earlier forms of religion would become merged, as rivers merge in the ocean. He was the Promised One, he stated, of all the prophets — Zoroaster, Moses, Jesus and Muhammad — the Divine Manifestation, in whose era the reign of peace on earth would actually be established. Though the impoverished peasants and city dwellers of Persia accepted Baha'Allah on his own terms, he was a serious threat to the established forms of religion, and the mullahs forced him to flee for his life. He went first to Baghdad, then to Constantinople, to Adrianople and finally to Acre (then called Akkah), on the Mediterranean coast, where he was imprisoned. He died in 1892, after making many converts in his travels.

The movement was no longer called Babism, but the Baha'i

Faith, after Baha'Allah. It was now his son's turn to take over. The son, Abdul Baha, was also imprisoned but was released in 1908. He went immediately to Europe and America, where he introduced Baha'i, enjoying a fine harvest of people from all faiths and none. Abdul Baha died in 1921, passing on the mantle of leadership to his eldest grandson, Shogi Effendi, as First Guardian of the Faith and interpreter of the teachings. The Effendi reorganized the administrative structure of Baha'i, making the movement a true reflection of Baha'Allah's teachings for a world order.

In the century and a third since the Bab first proclaimed his mystical, ecstatic view of a new age, his original doctrines, so fervent and emotional, have undergone a gradual diminution as they have moved from the Middle East to the West. No longer are mystical, ritual or theological beliefs paramount; instead simplicity, social-mindedness and positive thinking are stressed. The primary vision is one of God, even though men may call Him by different names, and of one world attained through a world religion — that is, through the Baha'i Faith. The world begins with the individual, who must have high moral standards and a new basis of belief. Since there is but one God, all manifestations of God have each taught the same religious faith, developing and adapting it to meet historical and cultural demands. The unfolding of religion from age to age is called "progressive revelation." Baha'Allah is the Manifestation of God for our time. Humanity is one: people of different races must enjoy equal educational and economic opportunities, equal access to decent living conditions and equal responsibilities. No race or nation is superior to another. The Baha'i Faith has no priesthood or professional clergy; there are no rites or rituals. Services are merely readings from Baha'i and other world scriptures. The Faith has a large membership in the United States. The Baha'i temple at

Wilmette, Illinois (near Chicago), is world-famous, and many non-Baha'i visit it. Baha'is try to make the pilgrimage to the Bab's grave in the Holy Land, for next to it is also the grave of Baha'Allah, the bones of both prophets still awaiting the final merging of all mankind into one faith. Baha'i beliefs are simple and positive.

"All the prophets of God proclaim the same faith. Ye are the fruits of one tree and the leaves of one branch," say the inscriptions cut into the walls of the great Baha'i temples. "So powerful is unity's light that it can illuminate the whole earth." And admonitions to lead a life of probity and good behavior follow: "Breathe not the sins of others so long as thou art thyself a sinner. The best beloved of all things in My sight is Justice; turn not away therefrom if thou desirest Me," for "My love is My stronghold; he that entereth therein is safe and secure. Make mention of Me on My earth that in My heaven I may remember thee."

Current Baha'i doctrines are not likely to arouse the peasants and slum dwellers of Mideast cities. One wonders how the original mystical call of the Bab, the Gateway of Divine Revelation, would be received today, not among impoverished Shi'a awaiting an eschatological call, but among affluent Westerners.

THEOSOPHY

In the early 1870s a Buddha incarnation, Tsong-kah-pa, appeared to a Russian-born woman, Madame Helena Petrovna Blavatsky (she was then in her forties), to inform her that she had been selected to help save the world. Moreover, Madame Blavatsky — commonly called H.P.B. by her disciples — had attained such high spirited development in her previous lives that she had acquired the occult power known as tulku among Tibetans — that is, she was divinely incarnated. The Buddha Tsong-kha-pa said she could temporarily and self-consciously remove her own ego-consciousness and permit his influence to act through her. He

[139]

The leading Baha'i temple in the United States is that at Wilmette, a Chicago suburb. Thirty-three years in the building, it is a symbol of the Baha'i Faith, with nine sides, a stipulation laid down in Baha'i teachings. Nine is the largest single number, and in Baha'i doctrines symbolizes comprehensiveness, oneness and unity.

Abdul Baha, son of Baha' Allah, the founder of the Baha'i Faith, took over the movement upon his father's death in 1892. He was immediately imprisoned by the Turks for his unorthodox religious views. On his release in 1908, he introduced the Baha'i Faith to Europe and the United States, with considerable success.

also informed her that she would work under the direction of two Adepts, Mahatma Marya and Mahatma Koot Hoomi, known later as Mahatma M. and Mahatma K. H., who resided in the Himalayas. On the evening of September 7, 1875, seventeen people gathered in H.P.B.'s rooms, ostensibly to hear a lecture by an architect named Felt on "The Lost Canon of Proportion of the Egyptians." Felt's lecture was anything but prosaic. He soon made the point that the Egyptian priests who built the ancient temples were "Adepts in magical science and had the power to evoke and employ the spirits of the elements." These powers were still extant, he hinted, and by certain magic formulae of the Egyptians he could transform his mind so that he, too, could see certain occult elements. After this, Madame Blavatsky rose to inform her friends that there is an Ageless Wisdom, the thread of which can be traced through all cultures and mythologies, through religion, science, and philosophy, as beautifully suggested by the study of these disciplines. With an American, her partner in spiritualist performances, Colonel H. S. Olcott, and fourteen other interested people, H.P.B. began the Theosophical Society that night.

H.P.B. was a curious figure. Her friends stood in awe of her occult powers, which she used sparingly but effectively, and only when there was a reason, not merely to entertain the curious. Her disciples reported many examples. One of the early members, A. P. Sinnett, a journalist living in India, reported that occult temple bells would ring anytime H.P.B. wished, without any sign of actual bells in the area. At one point she produced a cup and saucer to match a crockery set at a picnic when unexpected guests arrived. But her most puzzling powers — they are called siddhis in India by Hindus and Buddhists — involved her correspondence by spiritual means with her two masters, the Himalayan Mahatmas. She passed on letters from Sinnett and others to both Mahatmas by "thought transference" and received answers in colloquial English ("by the bye" is a typical example) impressed *in* the grain of rice paper. (The original letters, along with the cup and saucer and other mementos, are now in the British Museum.)

Whether or not H.P.B. was in tune with certain aspects of the higher world each individual alone must decide. She herself stated that "the Buddha left the regions of the Western Paradise to incarnate himself in Tsong-kha-pa in consequence of the great degradation into which his secret doctrines had fallen." She revealed that the world was now under the guidance of the Adept Brothers, the Mahatma M. and the Mahatma K. H., who were liberated souls and had crossed the "ocean of births and deaths" but had remained "in incarnation to help the world on its upward path." Also, the Adepts were "highly evolved men, living men," for whom H.P.B. was agent and from whom she received a mandate to establish a nucleus of occultism in the West.

The period in which H.P.B. made her announcement was one in which many Westerners were beginning to feel disenchanted with the traditional Christianity in which most of them had been raised. Many intellectuals and well-educated people were looking for other spiritual sustenance, and the East had certain attractions. Much scholarship in Eastern religions, sciences, literature, customs and art was being done, and a number of documents, previously unknown, were being published through the auspices of such impressive institutions as Harvard, Oxford and Cambridge. A small Western elite fell in love with H.P.B. and Theosophy.

In 1879 headquarters of the Society were transferred from New York to Bombay, and four years later they were permanently established at Adyar, a small town now a suburb of Madras, on the southeastern Indian coast. Meanwhile, H.P.B. continued to pick up converts, including some among the Indians. The Society today has centers in some sixty countries but is barred from all

Communist lands except Yugoslavia. Though H.P.B. was the founder and the guiding spirit of Theosophy, Olcott was named its first president, to be followed by a dynamic Englishwoman, Annie Besant, who renounced her citizenship, joined the freedom movement against the British and became an Indian national; she was elected president of the Indian National Congress in 1918. It was during this period (until Besant's death in 1933) that the Theosophists functioned with the greatest élan. J. Krishnamurti, then a young man, was being groomed as a prospective Theosophy leader, but he suddenly left the Society, rejecting its doctrines; however, the Society continues to publish some of his works. There have been other schisms and divisions, the most important of which was led by Dr. Rudolf Steiner after an argument with Annie Besant; Steiner formed the Anthroposophical Society in 1912.

What Theosophy teaches is based upon certain basic texts of esoteric lore received by H.P.B. from the Adept Brothers, which have been written down for publication. The key works are her *The Secret Doctrine*, *Isis Unveiled*, *The Key to Theosophy* and *The Mahatma Letters to A. P. Sinnett*. There was much reworking of basic themes during the early years, and three fundamental tenets were at last established which are at the core of Theosophical doctrine, no matter how esoteric:

> To form a nucleus of the Universal Brotherhood of Humanity, without distinction of race, creed, sex, caste or color.
> To encourage the study of Comparative Religion, Philosophy and Science.
> To investigate unexplained laws of Nature and the powers latent in man.

These deceptively simple objectives hide a highly elaborate occult theory of the Divine and man, which H.P.B. stated in 1888 and elaborated upon in later years. There is

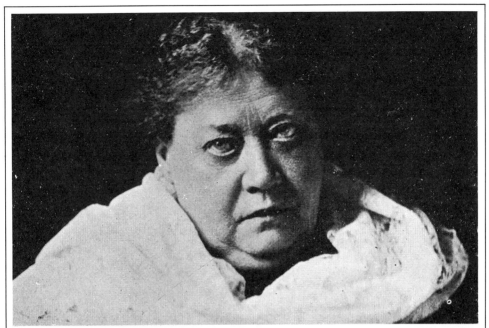

Helena Petrovna Blavatsky—"HPB" to her devotees—formally founded Theosophy in New York in November, 1875, in company with an American, H.S. Olcott. The Englishwoman Annie Besant brought the Society to its greatest success in the early years of this century. Here she is accompanied by the young Indian, J. Krishnamurti, whom the Theosophists saw as a divine incarnation. However, appalled by their excessive adulation of him, Krishnamurti broke with the Society.

ONE LIFE, eternal, invisible, yet omnipresent, without beginning or end, the one self-existing Reality.

Basic to this is the concept of

The fundamental identity of all Souls with the Universal Over-Soul, the latter being itself an aspect of the Unknown Root; and the obligatory pilgrimage for every Soul—a spark of the former—through the Cycle of Incarnation, or Necessity, in accordance with Cyclic and Karmic Law, during the whole term.

Madame Blavatsky believed that man was identical with the Universal Over-Soul, which is an aspect of the Unknown Root. However, despite this identity of every soul with the Over-Soul, the One Divine Consciousness, every individual is embarked on a pilgrimage and is governed by the law of karma, of action and reaction, cause and effect. By the process of reincarnation, each one is evolving in an ever-increasing spiral toward a state of complete "unfoldment." Man is a god in the becoming, a miniature universe, a microcosm of the Macrocosm, his potentialities beyond his own imagining. All are links in an endless chain of existence, with no apparent beginning and no apparent end.

Blavatsky stated—according to what the Mahatmas told her—that there is a Septenary Law guiding the world. This means that there are seven primordial rays emanating from the One, seven basic forces in nature, seven principles or differentiations of matter which form seven planes of existence. Correspondingly there are seven states of consciousness. Man is a seven-petalled lotus, reflecting the seven divine rays. Also, seven root races represent the development of mankind from a primitive being with only a sense of hearing (the second added was the sense of touch, and so on) to the present, through a kind of retracing of the evolutionary stage in which the skeleton develops and the senses of speech, sight, "mentality" and so on are added. We are now in the fifth sub-race of the fifth root-race, which she defines as the Aryan, or Indo-European. Early Theosophical doctrines definitely put the white man ahead of the various black, brown, yellow and red peoples, and these racial theories have haunted the Society since. The sixth root-race will develop intuition and clairvoyance, and the seventh, the faculty of direct perception and clairaudience. By the time of the last of the root-races mankind will presumably be so highly developed and so sensitive that, in effect, it will be all part of the One, each individual intuitively knowing and understanding all others. But for the present, it has been the work of the Society to save "inferior" races, and it began many schools and other institutions to help people in lands which deprive them of even the basic human rights. In India, where untouchability is still a part of the caste system, the Theosophists founded at least five schools to educate the untouchables, who are denied a full part in ordinary life.

H.P.B. thought that within the Theosophical path which was open to the average person there was also an occult Way which was the privilege of the initiate, and which was not apparent to ordinary eyes. An inner circle was formed, the Esoteric Section, to practice the Ageless Wisdom by "the study of practical Occultism of Raja Yoga." That H.P.B. and her initiates achieved some success in occult practices is possible, for critics of the Theosophists attacked them for their powers. At the height of Theosophy's popularity, a hostile investigator, Hermann Keyserling, a noted German philosopher, wrote in 1919 of Annie Besant and C. W. Ledbetter, another leading member of the Society:

> There is no doubt that both of them are honest, and both assert that they possess possibilities of experience, some of which are known under abnormal conditions, most of which, however, are totally unknown; both of them declare that they have acquired these powers in course of practice.

Specifically about Annie Besant, Keyserling said:

As to Annie Besant, there is one thing of which I am certain: this woman controls her being from a centre which, to my knowledge, only very few men have ever attained to . . . Mrs. Besant controls herself—her powers, her thoughts, her feelings, her volitions—so perfectly that she seems to be capable of greater achievements than men of greater gifts.

The Tashi Lama is second only to the Dalai Lama among Tibetans. The two were exploited in the past by foreign powers, the Dalai Lama by the British and the Tashi Lama by the Chinese. The Tashi Lama is considered an incarnation of the Amitabha Buddha, one of five high Buddhas (Gautama Buddha is the one best known in the West). The Amitabha Buddha is "He of the Boundless Light." In 1975 the Theosophical Society, on the occasion of its one hundredth anniversary, announced that the true Tashi Lama, who died in 1937 (the current one is in their view a Chinese puppet), would be incarnated in the West to be the successful messenger of the Occult Brotherhood who will carry out the mandate of Tsong-kha-pa. A child, born in 1970, has inherited the soul of the true Tashi Lama. He must be sought out and tested before his acceptance, a process that requires a number of years. But somewhere on this earth, perhaps in Tibet or India, perhaps in your own home, is the next true Tashi Lama, awaiting to be revealed to the world.

INDEX

Page numbers for illustrations are in italics.

[149]